Vanessa Lewendon

Above: *Gary Brooker, keyboard player with Procol Harum, wrote many fine songs in partnership with Keith Reid.*

Hamlyn
London • New York • Sydney • Toronto

Musical consultant/ Series editor
Arthur Butterfield

Studio photographer
Mike Gee

Picture Credits
Front cover; Mike Gee; *Back cover;* courtesy Terry Lott/CBS Records (top right), London Features International; Pages 2-3, courtesy Terry Lott/CBS Records; Pages 4-5, courtesy Tom Sheehan/CBS Records; Page 50 courtesy CBS Records; Pages 10-11, courtesy Norlin Music (UK) Ltd. & Sampson Tyrrell Ltd.; Pages 56 & 61, Jazz Music Books; Page 9, courtesy Robert Morley & Co. Ltd.; Page 9, courtesy Yamaha Organs; Page 7, courtesy Whelpdale, Maxwell & Codd Ltd.; Pages 1, 6, 11 (bottom), 16, 17, 18, 19, 20, 22, 23, 26, 30, 31, 32, 33, 34, 37, 38, 39, 40, 42, 43, 53, 54, 58 & 60, London Features International; Page 13, courtesy Charisma Records; Page 47, courtesy Decca Record Company.

Pop consultant:
Bob Kenrick

Designed and produced by Intercontinental Book Productions

Printed in Spain.
Deposito Legal B-12.054-1979

Left: *The widely acclaimed jazz musician, Chick Corea, combined jazz and rock in his band Return to Forever.*

INTRODUCTION

YOU MUST think the keyboard is for you, or you would not be reading this book right now. If so, you're in luck. You're really one of a happy few. Think how many guys and girls claim to be able to tickle the guitar strings a little; or blow the guts out of a harmonica; or even make noises on the cornet and big trombone. But keyboard kings are rarer now than they used to be. And too often the old joanna or the costly organ lies neglected in the corner while the party dies for want of a player.

Perhaps it's the usual array of frightening self-teaching manuals that puts people off. But actually playing the piano or the organ is much easier than most people think, as you'll soon see. It doesn't matter whether the instrument you're itching to get your hands on is an old upright hand-me-down piano or a £3,000 Hammond organ, the basics are the same. With what you learn from this book you'll be able to play all kinds of keyboards.

Keyboard instruments can be very costly. But don't despair – you can still pick up a second-hand piano for less than £50. It will probably need tuning, which may cost you another £8 or £10, but unlike a guitar or a fiddle, you won't have to retune it each time you want to play. Before setting out to buy an instrument, ask a friend who knows something about such things to go along with you. He may be able to save you a fortune. But even so, keyboard instruments live, if not forever, at least for a very long time.

Sadly, you will not be able to get away without any practice at all. Half an hour's work a day on the instrument will do far more good than eight hours once a fortnight. If you work faithfully at the few exercises in this book, you will soon be able to sort out your fingers from your thumbs, and in next-to-no-time you'll find yourself playing the pieces.

If you study the following pages carefully you will be able to play a keyboard instrument without any knowledge of music whatsoever. But there is also some simple music theory in the book. Learning music is easy: it is not nearly as difficult as learning another language or learning to type or to drive a car, for instance. After all, you will have to get to know the notes of the keyboard and how to use them. With this knowledge you're well on the way to becoming a real 'musician'.

Left: *Herbie Hancock is another American jazz musician who has successfully fused jazz with rock styles.*

KINDS OF KEYBOARDS

THERE ARE many different kinds of keyboards. In case you haven't made up your mind which kind you'd like to play, here's a brief rundown on the more popular ones that are used today.

Piano

The most popular of all is the piano. It came originally from Italy and was known as the *pianoforte* ('soft-loud'). It was so named because it could play both soft and loud tones – a feature that the earlier keyboard instruments lacked. The piano has a number of steel strings stretched across a sounding board. These are made to sound when hit by small felt-covered hammers, which are brought into action when the black and white keys are played.

The three types of acoustic piano are the *grand,* the *baby grand,* and the *upright.*

Opposite: *Singer and pianist Nina Simone.*
Below: *An upright piano, ideal for home use.*

Electric piano

The electric piano is smaller than its acoustic cousin and has fewer keys. Instead of strings it has a system of electrical connections which are wired to an amplifier. There is a volume pedal, and the sound is adjusted by means of knobs. It can be used effectively with all types of popular music.

Right: *Electric piano of the type widely used by bands in the early 1960s.*

Organ

Among the many kinds of organs on the market, the *reed, pipe* and *electric* are the most common. In both reed and pipe organs, air is forced through a series of pipes of differing lengths to produce the notes. In the electric organ, rotating wheels, called oscillators, produce electric charges to provide the basic *pitch* (height or depth) of the notes. Controls called 'stops' and 'tabs' enable the player to alter the sound of the instrument.

Top left: *Single manual electric organ.*
Top right: *The complexities of an electric organ.*
Centre left: *Close-up of the instrument showing the tab that can be used.*
Centre right: *The swell pedal, for volume.*
Bottom left: *A dual manual electric organ.*
Bottom right: *Bass pedals, for the deep notes.*

Harpsichord

That ancient instrument, the harpsichord, is enjoying something of a revival thanks to the popularity of electrically aided folk music. The harpsichord looks like a miniature grand piano. Its light, metallic sound is produced by a plectrum which plucks at the strings, and which replaces the hammers in the piano. On the acoustic harpsichord the tone can't be altered, but electric instruments have pick-ups instead of a sounding board; as a result, the tone can be changed by means of switches.

Harmonium

The harmonium works in the same way as a mouth organ. Air is blown across a series of reeds (metal tongues) causing them to vibrate. Air comes from bellows that are electrically operated or worked by pedals. Harmoniums also have stops in an attempt to give them the same range of expression as organs. The harmonium has been used successfully in soft-rock music.

Below left: *Harpsichord with two keyboards.*
Below: *The harmonium, predecessor to the organ.*

Synthesizer

Although not strictly speaking a keyboard instrument, the synthesizer is usually used in conjunction with an electronic keyboard. Synthesizers are completely electronic instruments on which the operator can produce the sounds of other instruments or create entirely new sounds.

Below left: *Small synthesizer with keyboard.*
Below: *Large synthesizer, with a close-up of the panel with mixer controls for different sounds.*

MEET YOUR KEYBOARD

A KEYBOARD is any instrument made up of black and white keys that form a pattern. The keyboard of an organ is called a *manual*.

Look at the picture above and you'll see that the white keys are placed at equal distances from each other, while the black keys are arranged in groups of twos and threes.

Start by pressing down the key at the far left of the keyboard and then press down each key in turn. Each one makes a slightly higher sound than the one before it. The height or depth of a sound is called its *pitch*.

The white keys take the names of the first seven letters of the alphabet: A B C D E F G. After G, you go back to A again, and the pattern is repeated many times. These letters are called *notes* when written in musical notation. You will find it much easier to play if you learn the names of the keys by heart. In this way you'll be able to pick out any note at once.

To help you find your way around the keyboard there is a landmark called *Middle C*. On the piano you'll find it in the middle of the keyboard – the white key just before the two black keys.

On the organ, whether single or double manual, Middle C might be found in a different position, as you can see from the picture at the top of the next page.

Generally speaking, all the notes to the *right* of Middle C are played with your *right* hand. All the notes to the *left* of Middle C are played with your *left* hand. With a dual manual organ, you play the top manual with your right hand and the bottom one with your left. These rules are sometimes broken or bent, but such variations merely go to make music all that much more interesting, as you'll find out for yourself before very long.

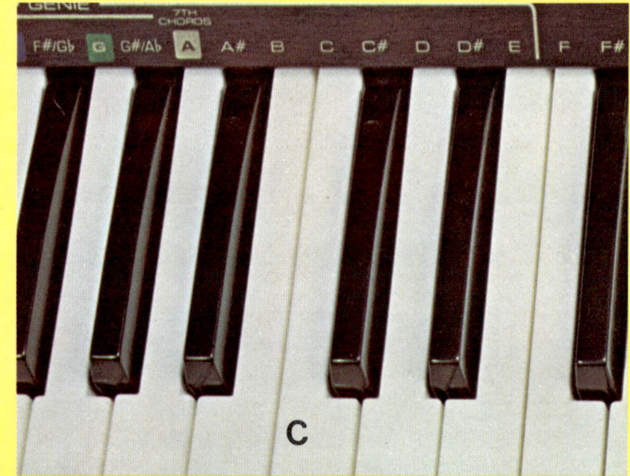

Top: *Large dual manual electric organ with built-in synthesizer; mainly for studio use.*
Above: *Middle C on the keyboard.*

The keyboard is divided into a series of *octaves*. An octave is made up of 12 keys (notes) – seven white keys and five black keys.

Each black key may be both a *sharp* or a *flat*. These are musical terms to define half steps (half tones) in the scale – something you need not worry about at this stage.

If you put your finger on one of the white keys and then count along for another seven keys, you'll find that you've arrived back at a key of the same letter as you started with, only an octave higher or lower in pitch. When you play two or more keys together at the same time, you get a fuller, richer sound. Such a combination of notes is called a *chord.*

So far you've heard about 'keys', with reference to the keys that make up the keyboard. But the word 'key' in music also describes the tones that make up a scale (or ladder). There are many different scales and all music is based on one or more of these scales.

Top: *Two manuals and Middle C on both.*
Above: *Right hand spanning the octave, C to C.*
Below: *Session pianist Rick Wakeman.*

SIT AND RAP

WHEN YOU first sit down at the keyboard, make sure that you are facing the middle of it. Relax – but stay upright. Don't get all hunched up over the keyboard, and don't lean against the back of the chair. Both attitudes will give you a backache before long. Put both feet on the floor and keep your legs uncrossed. This leaves your legs free to cope with the pedals.

Check your height at the keyboard. It should be such as to allow your elbows to be slightly higher than your wrists when playing. Keep the backs of your hands level and your fingers well rounded. You will then strike the keys with the fleshy tips of your fingers. This applies to your three middle fingers only – your little finger should be almost straight, and your thumb should rest on its side.

Keep your nails cut short; long nails get in the way and break. If you wear rings, it helps to take

Below, reading left to right from the top: *Wrong and right way to sit: picture 1 shows the player hunched over the keyboard; picture 2 shows her leaning back too far; picture 3 shows the correct posture. Pictures 4 and 5 show the correct positions of the legs and feet. Wrong and right hand positions: picture 6 shows the hand too arched; picture 7 shows the hand resting on the keyboard; pictures 8 and 9 show the correct placing of left and right hands.*

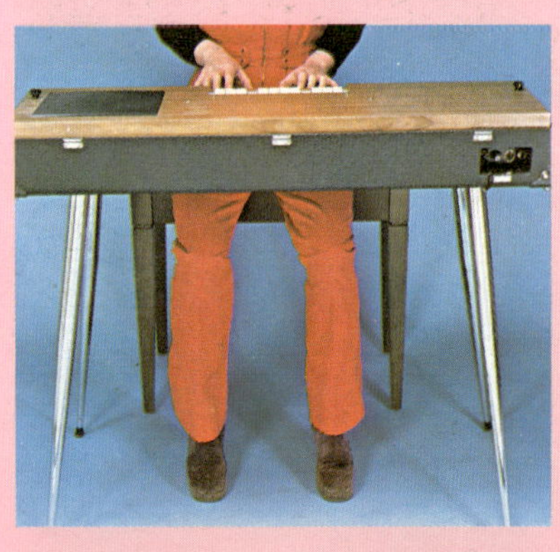
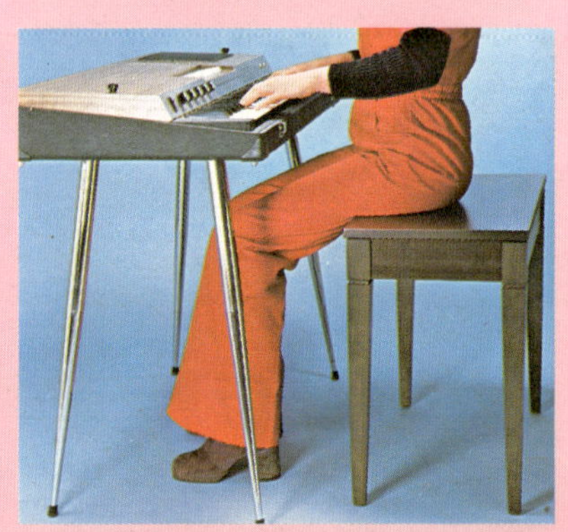

them off while playing; your fingers will feel much freer.

Here are a couple of useful starters in the way of exercise. Lay your arm, from elbow to wrist, on any flat surface, such as a table. Now draw your arm back from the wrist as high as you can and let your hand fall sharply back on to the table again.

Repeat this exercise several times with each arm in turn.

Now shift your arm to the edge of the table, as shown in the picture. Lift your hand to the level of your arm, then let it fall over the edge of the table again. Try it with each arm in turn, several times.

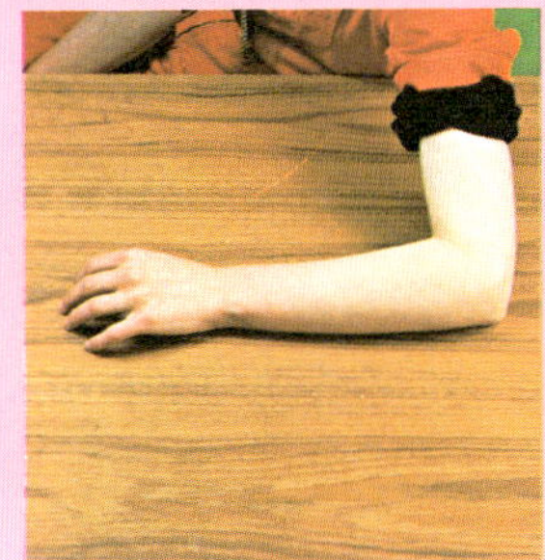

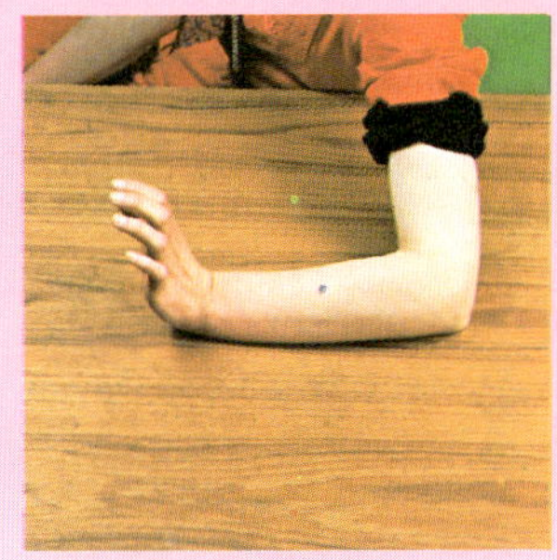

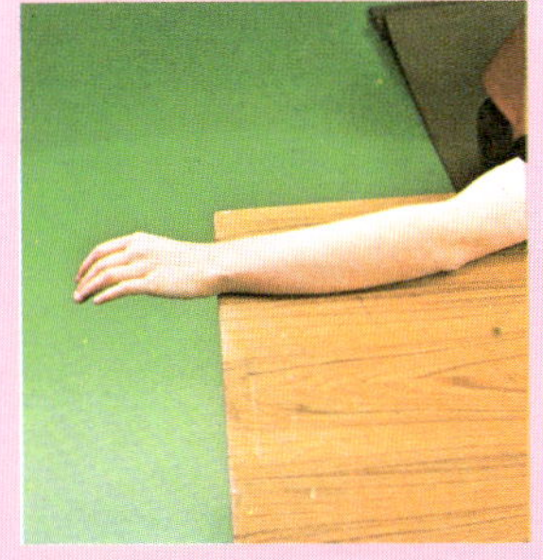

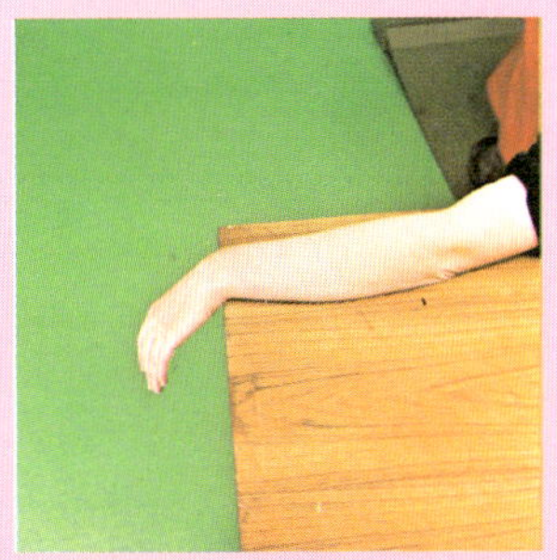

Right: *The two top pictures show the first hand exercise; the two below show the second exercise.*

Below: *Ex-Yes man Patrick Moraz brought sophistication to rock music.*

WHO NEEDS MUSIC?

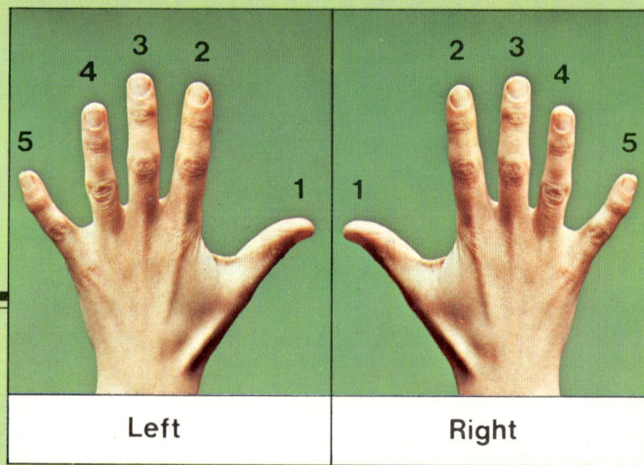

WOULD YOU believe that you can play at once without having to read a single note of music? I'll prove it to you.

First, let's number the fingers and thumbs of each hand from 1 to 5, starting with the thumb. Remember, you decide which finger you're going to use to play a particular note because there are no hard and fast rules about this in popular music. Even so, it still makes sense to use certain fingers with certain note progressions, otherwise you'll soon be in a muddle. Anyway, you'll find that, as you go along, the finger indications will only be used where they are absolutely necessary.

Now look at the Colour Code Chart at the foot of the page. You'll see that the keyboard is divided into octaves, and to make things clearer each octave has been given its own colour. Starting on Middle C, the white keys in the octave immediately to the right are coloured *green:* the white keys in the octave higher (farther to the right) are coloured *brown:* the white keys in the octave immediately to the left are *red:* the white keys in the octave lower (farther to the left) are *blue.*

The names of the notes are printed in black on these colours. The right hand normally plays the notes in the *green* and *brown* octaves, and the left hand in the *red* and *blue* octaves.

For a few pence, you can buy a packet of adhesive coloured paper shapes. Take out the appropriate colours, letter them as per the chart and stick them onto the correct keys of your keyboard. Once you become familiar with the keyboard you'll be able to dispense with this aid. These colours for the octaves also appear in the music tablature we will use, which is shown (in a simplified form) immediately below. You'll see that the hands have been marked *right* and *left* accordingly, and that there are three horizontal lines for each hand.

Right: the middle line is for notes in the *green* octave, and the top line for notes in the *brown* octave.
Left: the top line is for notes in the *red* octave, and the middle line for notes in the *blue* octave.

	Brown
Right	Green
	Fingering
	Red
Left	Blue
	Fingering

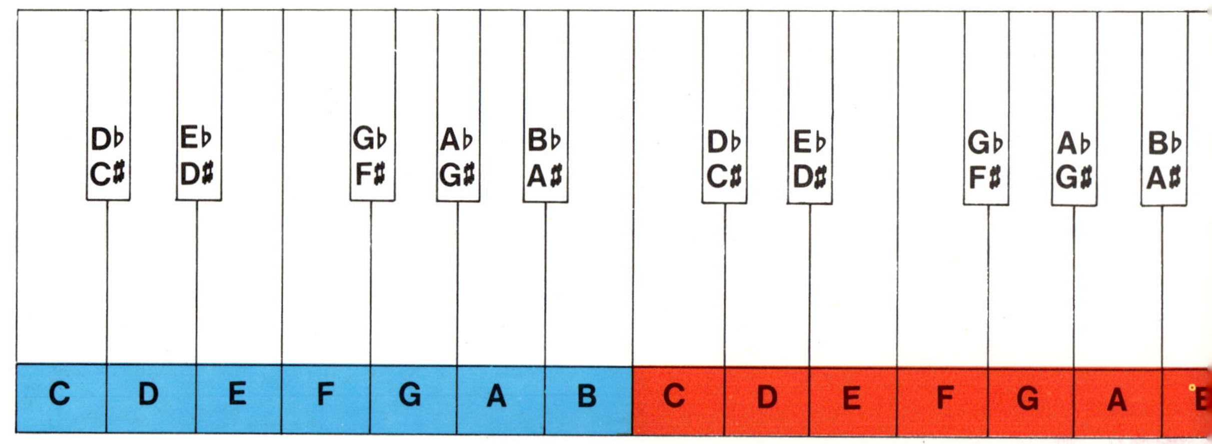

TAKE CARE: sometimes the right hand has to move down the keyboard to play in the *red* (left hand) octave, and the left hand has to move up to play in the *green* (right hand) octave.

Here you can see how the right hand goes down the keyboard to play notes in the *red* octave.
Similarly here you can see that the left hand has moved up the keyboard to play in the *green* octave.

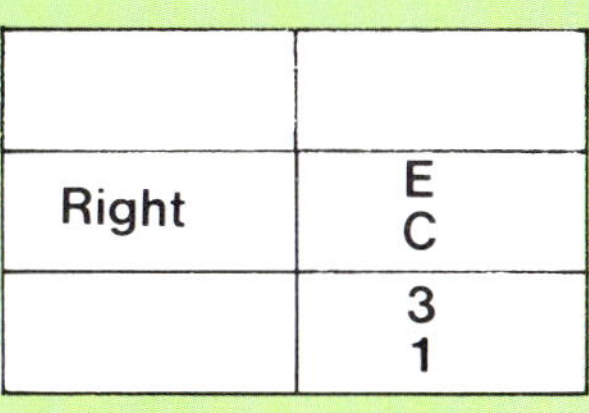

Right	Green	Red
Left	Red	Green

You've learned that the black notes are called sharps and flats. A black note to the *right* of a white note is a sharp: a black note to the *left* of a white note is a *flat.* Musicians use a kind of shorthand for these. Thus:

Sharp ♯ Flat ♭

Here are the names of all the black notes:

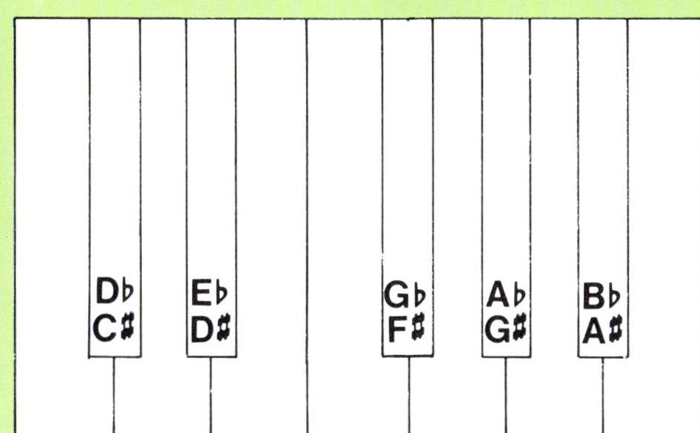

When written they will be on the colour of their octave but with a sharp or flat sign.

e.g. C ♯ E ♭

When you play a chord (like CE below) the notes will be written one on top of the other.

Right	E C
	3 1

Here is a breakdown of that chord. You play the C note of the green octave with the thumb of your right hand and the E note with the middle finger of the right hand.

As I am only using two lines per octave for each hand, there will be a lot of notes written on the same level. When a single note follows a chord it will be written on the same line as the lower half of the chord, as in the tablature below. The space between the two hands will be where the words are placed.

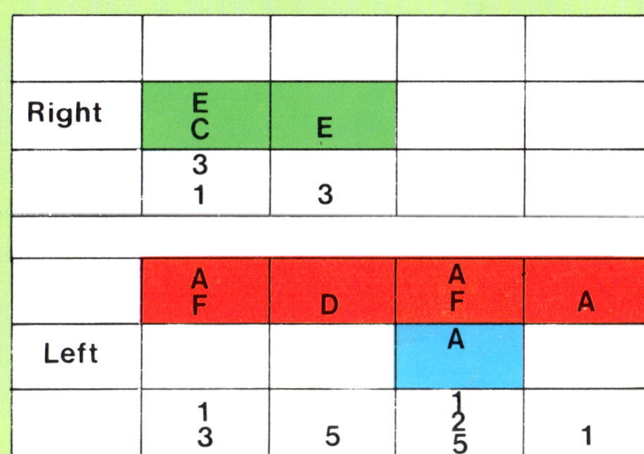

Right	E C	E		
	3 1	3		
	A F	D	A F	A
Left			A	
	1 3	5	1 2 5	1

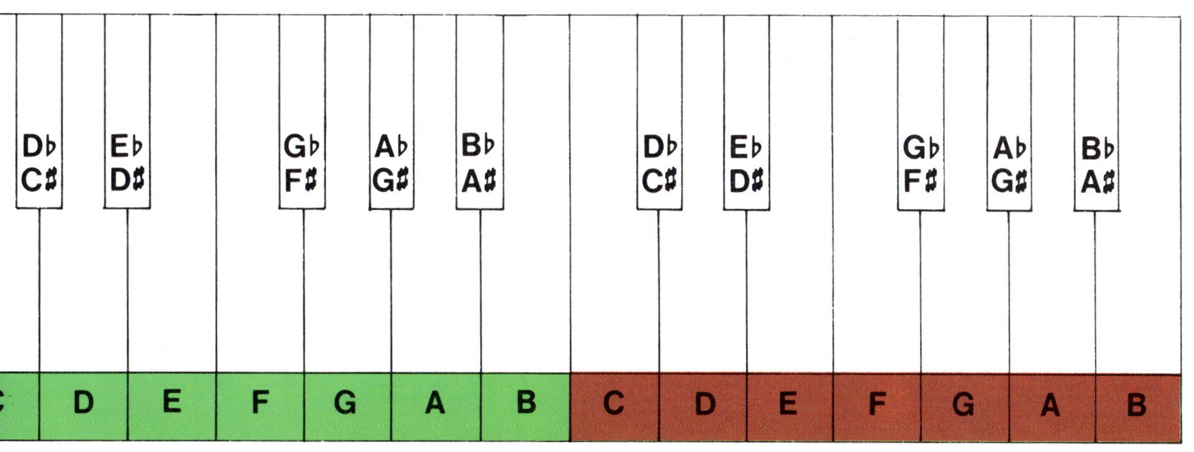

WARMING UP

NOW LET'S start using the colour chart. Here are a few simple exercises to get your fingers used to the keyboard. The exercises won't last long I can promise you! And remember that even the greatest pianists and organists had to start somewhere.

Try the exercise below with each hand in turn. When you feel ready for it, try the same exercise with both hands together. You'll notice that you're playing the same notes with each hand. Be warned: you'll rarely have it as easy as this in an actual piece of music. Usually each hand plays different notes.

By now you're no doubt dying to play your first tune so let's get cracking. The tunes that follow are all well known as most of them have been in the charts at one time.

You will find that after each song I have included the right hand written in normal music. This will enable someone who can read music to play the melody to you, if the song is unfamiliar. However do remember that the music is slightly different from the tablature, the former having been simplified for easy playing.

Opposite: *Keith Emerson was one of the first to popularize the Moog synthesizer.*
Right: *Richard Manuel sprang to fame with The Band, playing with Bob Dylan.*

Right	C	D	E	F	G	F	E	D	C
	1	2	3	4	5	4	3	2	1
Left	C	D	E	F	G	F	E	D	C
	5	4	3	2	1	2	3	4	5

Right	C	E	D	F	E	G	F	D	E	C
	1	3	2	4	3	5	4	2	3	1
Left	C	E	D	F	E	G	F	D	E	C
	5	3	4	2	3	1	2	4	3	5

AMAZING GRACE

THE FIRST piece is *Amazing Grace,* a traditional ballad tune that has become a favourite sacred song on both sides of the Atlantic. The words were written at the end of the 1700s by the ex-captain of a slave ship who penned them as a testimony to his conversion to Christianity.

The song, with its almost hymnlike phrases, builds up to a triumphant climax before dying away on a note of quiet confidence.

Versions of the song range from Doc Watson's stark, unaccompanied simplicity, through the fierce sincerity of Joan Baez and Judy Collins, to the martial sound of the pipers of the Royal Scots Dragoon Guards.

The right hand and left hand play single notes. Remember that in the tablature all the notes for the right hand are written *above* the lyrics, while those for the left hand are *below* the lyrics. The key is C major, which means that you play on the white notes only.

Right: *Singer-songwriter Judy Collins found success on both sides of the Atlantic with her version of* Amazing Grace.

	C	E	D	C	E	E	D	C		
G									A	G
1	3	5	4	3	5	5	4	3	2	1
A —	ma —	z —	i —	ng	grace	how —	—	sweet	the	sound
	C				C			F		C
	5				5			3		5

	C	E	D	C	E	F	G
G							
1	3	5	4	3	1	2	3
That	saved	a	—	—	wretch	like	me
C					C		G
5					5		3

E	G	E	D	C	E	E	D	C		
									A	G
3	5	3	2	1	3	3	2	1	3	1
I	once	w —	a —	s	lost	but —		now	I'm	found
	C				C			F		C
	5				5			3		5

	C	E	D	C	E	D	C
G							
1	3	5	4	3	5	4	3
Was	blind	but —			now	I	see.
	C				G		C
	5				3		5

2. 'Twas grace that taught my heart to fear,
And grace my fear relieved.
How precious did that grace appear,
The hour I first believed.

3. Through many dangers, toils and snares
We have already come.
'Twas grace that brought us safe thus far,
And grace will lead us home.

4. When we've been there ten thousand years,
Bright shining as the sun.
We've no less days to sing God's praise
Than when we first begun.

Above: *Alex Harvey used to end his stage performances with a piper playing* Amazing Grace.

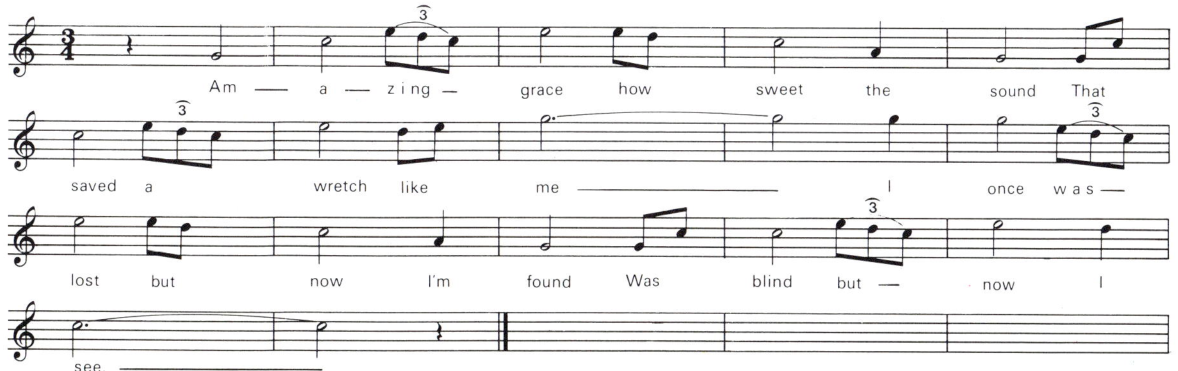

ON THE BEAT

AN IMPORTANT consideration in music is *time* – the speed at which you play a piece and the duration of each note in relation to the others.

The longest note (in time) in music is called a *whole note.* It lasts twice as long as a half note and four times as long as a quarter note. Correspondingly shorter notes are called eighths, sixteenths, thirty-seconds and so on. The names are American – they are more logical than the British names.

In conventional written music the notes and their respective duration are shown by a series of symbols. But as far as this book is concerned, you can forget about them.

All music is divided into *bars.* A bar is a group of notes separated from another group of the same duration by a vertical line. Duration is calculated by the number of beats in a bar and their respective value in time. At the beginning of each piece of music you will find two numbers, written one above the other and looking like a fraction. The top figure tells you how many beats there are in the bar and the bottom figure tells you the value of each beat.

Opposite: *Peter Gabriel formed and led the band Genesis before becoming a solo artist.*

There are other *time signatures* as these fractions are called. For example 3/8 means that there are 3 beats in the bar and that the value of each beat is an *eighth* note.

But in this book you will encounter only 4/4, 3/4 and 2/4 time signatures. Now let's get to know the notes and their value more fully.

From the chart below you will see that a *whole* note is played on the first count and held for the four counts. A *half* note is held for two counts and a *quarter* note for one count. Then there are two *eighth* notes per count and so on.

It is really simple arithmetic; depending on

<table>
<tr><td colspan="8">1</td><td colspan="8">2</td><td colspan="8">3</td><td colspan="8">4</td></tr>
<tr><td colspan="8">WHOLE NOTE</td><td colspan="8"></td><td colspan="8"></td><td colspan="8"></td></tr>
<tr><td colspan="8">HALF NOTE</td><td colspan="8"></td><td colspan="8">HALF NOTE</td><td colspan="8"></td></tr>
<tr><td colspan="8">QUARTER NOTES</td><td colspan="8">QUARTER NOTES</td><td colspan="8">QUARTER NOTES</td><td colspan="8">QUARTER NOTES</td></tr>
<tr><td colspan="4">EIGHTH NOTES</td><td colspan="4">EIGHTH NOTES</td><td colspan="4">EIGHTH NOTES</td><td colspan="4">EIGHTH NOTES</td><td colspan="4">EIGHTH NOTES</td><td colspan="4">EIGHTH NOTES</td><td colspan="4">EIGHTH NOTES</td><td colspan="4">EIGHTH NOTES</td></tr>
<tr><td colspan="2">16th</td><td colspan="2">16th</td><td colspan="2">16th</td><td colspan="2">16th</td><td colspan="2">16th</td><td colspan="2">16th</td><td colspan="2">16th</td><td colspan="2">16th</td><td colspan="2">16th</td><td colspan="2">16th</td><td colspan="2">16th</td><td colspan="2">16th</td><td colspan="2">16th</td><td colspan="2">16th</td><td colspan="2">16th</td><td colspan="2">16th</td></tr>
<tr><td>32</td><td>32</td><td>32</td><td>32</td><td>32</td><td>32</td><td>32</td><td>32</td><td>32</td><td>32</td><td>32</td><td>32</td><td>32</td><td>32</td><td>32</td><td>32</td><td>32</td><td>32</td><td>32</td><td>32</td><td>32</td><td>32</td><td>32</td><td>32</td><td>32</td><td>32</td><td>32</td><td>32</td><td>32</td><td>32</td><td>32</td><td>32</td></tr>
</table>

the time-signature, each bar can have any combination of notes as long as they all add up to the right number of beats in the bar. Thus, a 4/4 time signature could be made up of several different notes, or just a whole note, as shown below.

However 3/4 and 2/4 cannot have a *whole* note but they can have any of the other notes.

So presuming you understand all this, how will it be written? Well, like the chart at the bottom of the page.

First of all we have the *BAR-LINE* – a dark line vertically written. Then we will have slightly

1	2	3		4
half note		$\frac{1}{8}$	$\frac{1}{8}$	quarter

1	2	3	4
whole note			

lighter lines, either 2, 3 or 4 per bar to show the number of beats. We will call these lighter lines *DIVISIONS.*

Then depending on the *value* of each note, there will be lines called *SUB-DIVISIONS* which will act as a guide.

Thus, if a *DIVISION* is divided into 4 *SUB-DIVISIONS,* the value of these will be sixteenth notes. (On the chart, D E C D in the right hand is made up of sixteenth notes.)

Now obviously instead of *whole notes* and so on written in the spaces, you will see the letter names of the keyboard, as in *Amazing Grace.*

Above: *Tony Banks was a founder member of Genesis, formed at Charterhouse School.*

Sometimes in music a note is dotted and this means that it is held for half the value in time again. However, I have not dotted any notes but instead I have left the appropriate space, which will be coloured in. And that makes up the completed notation.

Take Note: If you are playing say a half note on the right hand and eighth notes in the left hand, the first letter of each hand must be played together.

1	2		3	4	1				2	3		4
			C		D	E	C	D				
C	A	B							G	A		G E
1	3	4	5		2	3	1	2	3	4		3 1
LYRICS												
									C	E	A	G
G			E	G	D		G					
3			5	3	4		3		1	5	3	4

MORNING HAS BROKEN

Morning Has Broken was written by Eleanor Farjeon and became a big hit for Cat Stevens, who arranged and recorded it.

This is another piece in C major, but this time you've got three beats to the bar. Try to put the accent on the first note of each bar.

Below: *Guitarist and songwriter Cat Stevens.*

			C			D					
C	E	G		G E	G E		A F	A F	B	A G	D B
1	3	4	5	5 3			4 2				
Morn —	ing	Has	Brok —	—	—	en			Like	the first	
			C			D			G		
			5			4			2		

A	F C	F C	G	E C	E G	C	D	E C	G	E B	E B
morn —	—	—	ing,			Black	bird	has	spok —	—	—
			C			C					
F									E		
3			1			1			3		

A	E C	E C	G D	D	D A	D	B G	B G	D	D B	D B
– en			Like	the	first	bird.					
A			D			G			G		
1											

			C								
G	E C	G E C		A F	A F	A	F C	F C	G	E C	D
Praise	for	the	sing —	—	—	ing,			Praise	for	the
C			F			F			C		

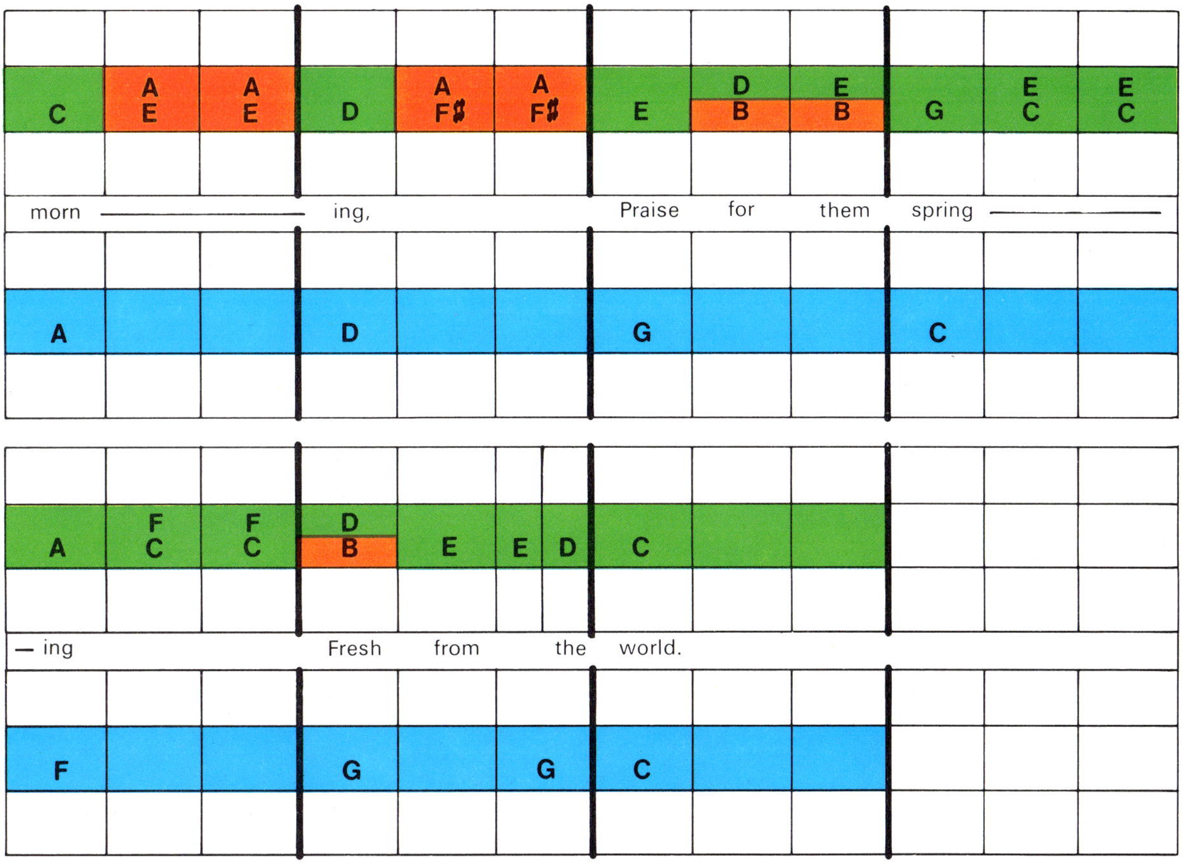
C A E A E D A F♯ A F♯ E D B E B G E C E C
morn — ing, Praise for them spring —
A D G C
A F C F C D B E E D C
— ing Fresh from the world.
F G G C

2. Sweet the rain's new fall,
Sunlit from heaven,
Like the first dew-fall
On the first grass.
Praise for the sweetness of the wet garden,
Sprung in completeness where his feet pass.

3. Mine is the sunlight,
Mine is the morning,
Born of the one light
Eden saw play.
Praise with elation,
Praise every morning,
Gods re-creation of the new day.

REPEAT FIRST VERSE

Morn—ing has brok — en Like the first morn —
— ing, Black bird has spok — en Like the first
bird. Praise for the sing — ing,
Praise for the morn — ing, Praise for them spring —
— ing Fresh from the world.

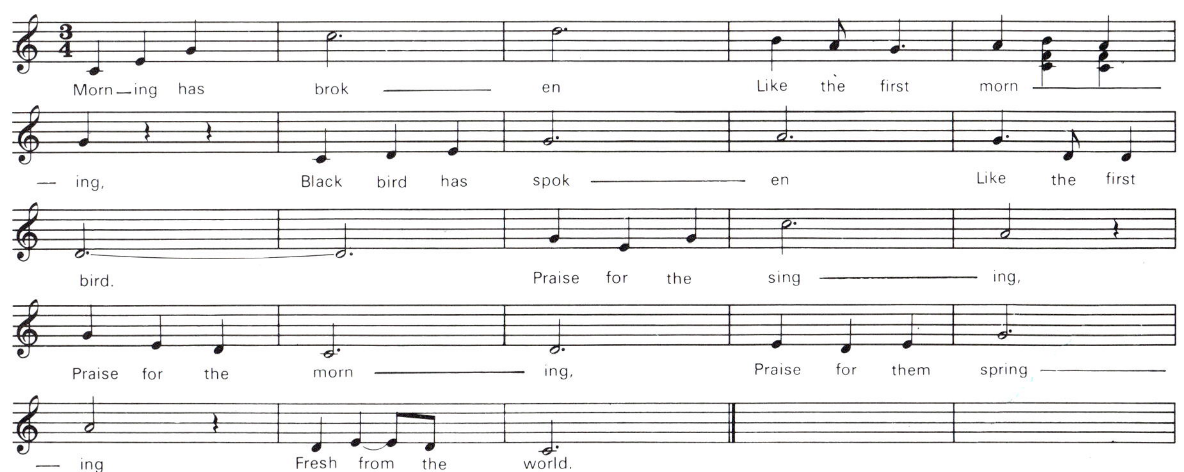

Early Morning Rain

GORDON LIGHTFOOT wrote and recorded *Early Morning Rain* in the 1960s.

This is the first piece you've come across that uses black notes. It is in D major, which means that you'll be playing an F sharp and a C sharp.

You've got another colour to cope with here too. In the *left* hand, a note on a *pink* background should be played in the octave below the blue one. Notes in the pink octave will add a deeper, richer sound to your playing.

Below: *Singer-songwriter Gordon Lightfoot's song* Early Morning Rain *has been recorded by numerous artists.*

		A F♯	A F♯	A F♯	A F♯	A F♯	G E	F♯ D	A	E C♯		E C♯
		3 1		3 1			5 3	4 2				
		In	the	ear —	ly	morn —		in'	rain			
	F♯											
D	A			D		D			A		E	
5	1 5			5		5			3		5	

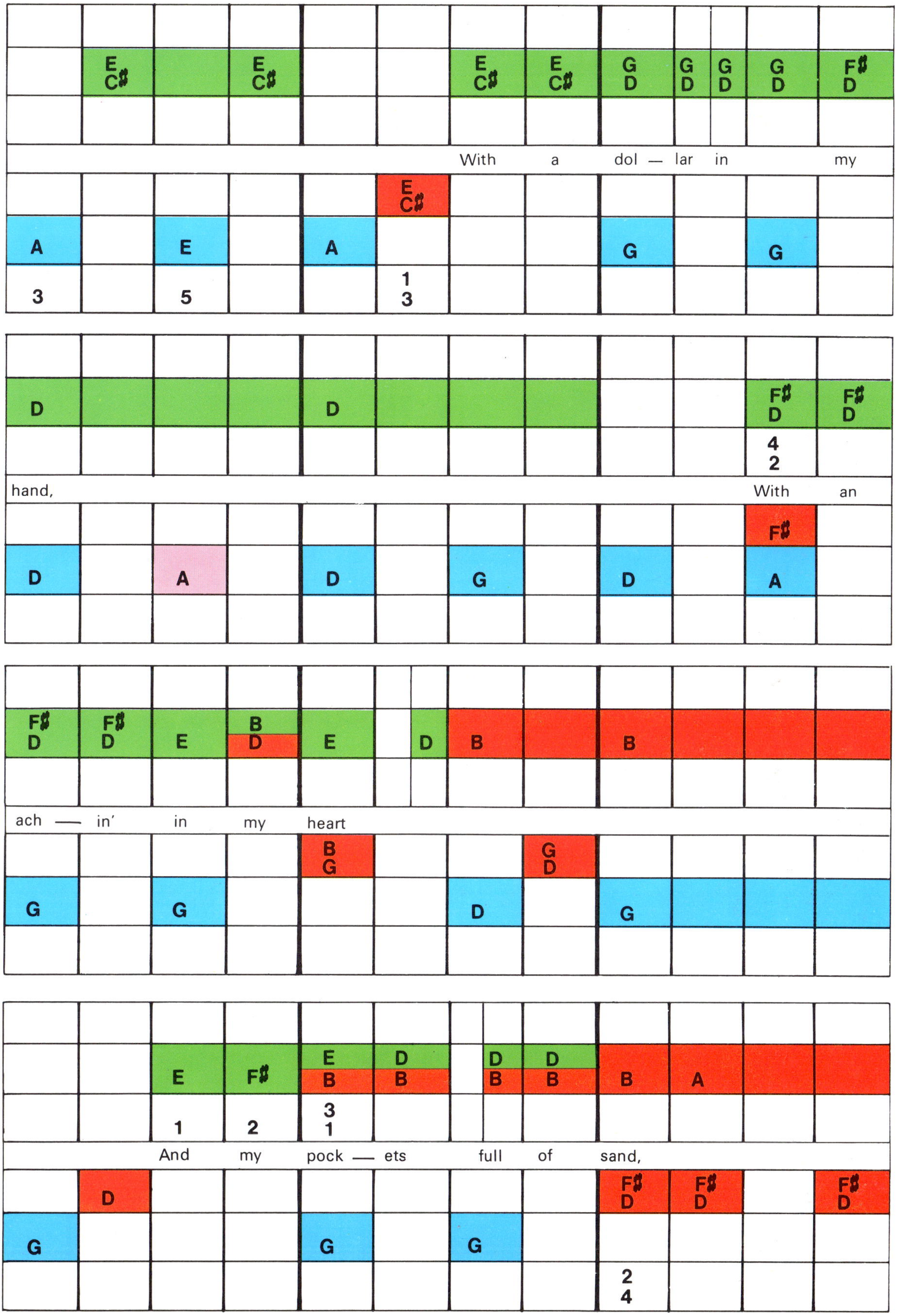

	E C♯		E C♯			E C♯	E C♯	G D	G D / G D	G D	F♯ D
						With	a	dol —	lar in		my
					E C♯						
A		E		A				G		G	
3		5			1 3						

D				D						F♯ D	F♯ D
										4 2	
hand,										With	an
										F♯	
D		A		D		G		D		A	

F♯ D	F♯ D	E	B D	E	/ D	B		B			
ach —	in'	in	my	heart							
				B G			G D				
G		G				D		G			

		E	F♯	E B	D B	/ D B	D B	B	A		
		1	2	3 1							
		And	my	pock —	ets	full	of	sand,			
	D							F♯ D	F♯ D		F♯ D
G				G		G					
								2 4			

A A A B D D

I'm a lo —— ng way from

F♯ D B G D

D G D D D

2
4

E D B B E B E B

home, ——————

And I

B G G G D G D D

D G D G

G E G E G E A E F♯ D E D A D A B

miss my loved ones so.

A A D A D G

A F♯ A F♯ A F♯ A F♯ A F♯ G E F♯ D A E C♯ E C♯

In the ear —— ly morn — in' rain,

F♯

D A D D A E

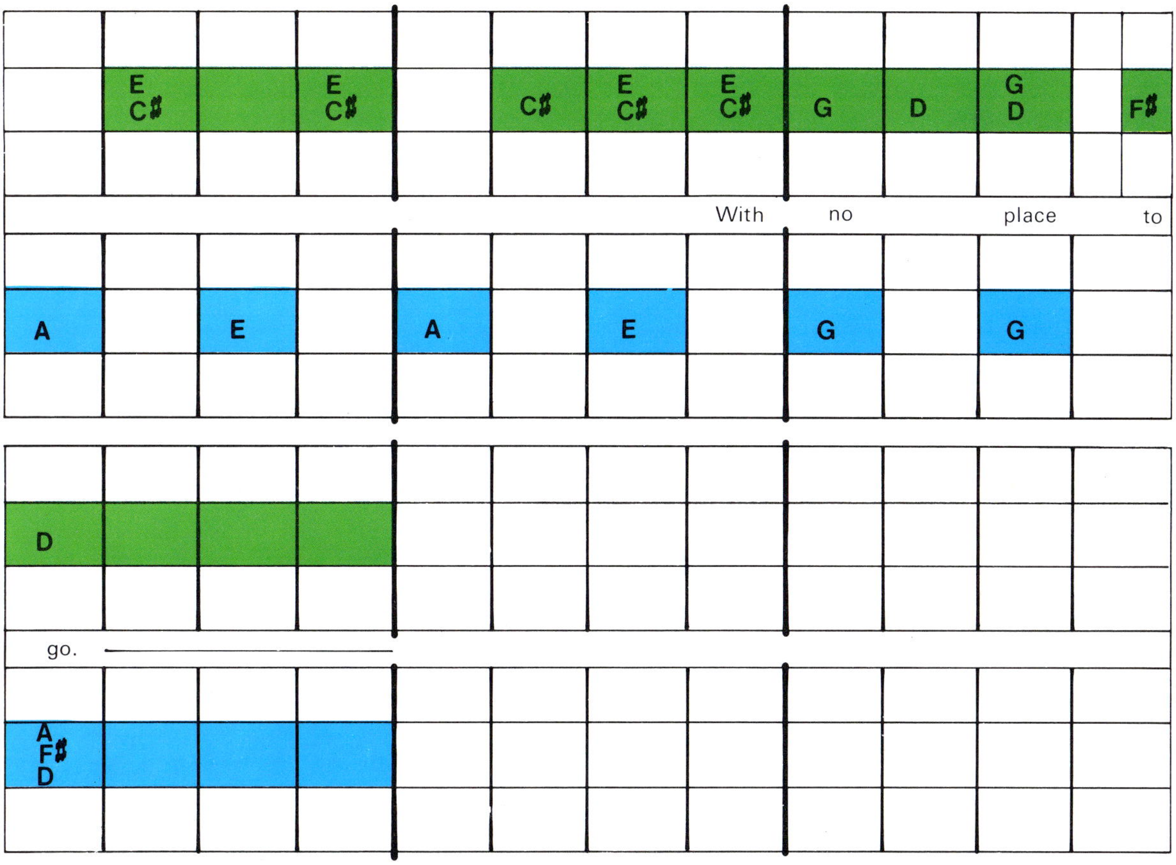

	E C#		E C#		C#	E C#	E C#	G	D	G D		F#
							With	no		place		to
A		E		A		E		G		G		

D											
go. ___											
A F# D											

2. Out on runway number nine
Big seven-o-seven set to go,
But I'm stuck here in the grass
Where the cold wind blows.
Now the liquor tasted good,
And the women all were fast,
Well, there she goes, my friend,
She's rollin' now at last.

3. Hear the mighty engines roar,
See the silver bird on high,
She's away and westward bound,
Far above the clouds she'll fly,
Where the mornin' rain don't fall,
And the sun always shines,
She'll be flyin' o'er my home
In about three hours' time.

4. This old airport's got me down,
It's no earthly good to me,
'Cause I'm stuck here on the ground
As cold and drunk as I can be.
You can't jump a jet plane
Like you can a freight train,
So I'd best be on my way
In the early mornin' rain.

MAKING A CHORD

ALTHOUGH WE called two notes played together a 'chord', you haven't really started to play proper chords yet. So here is something about them and how you can learn to build them for yourself.

Chords are made up of three or more notes played together. They are used to accompany the melody and give depth to a piece of music, and are played in various ways according to the mood of the music. If you want a heavy chord, you press down suddenly and with force. For a softer sound, you press slowly with a certain amount of restraint.

The degree of difference in pitch between notes is called an *interval,* and is measured by means of tones and half tones in the scale. (This is merely another way of describing steps and half steps in a musical stepladder.)

In the picture (top right) you'll see that the interval between any two white keys with a black key between them is one whole tone. There is also an interval of a whole tone between any two black keys that are separated by a white key. Where two white keys jostle each other cheek by jowl without being divided by a black key, the interval is a half tone.

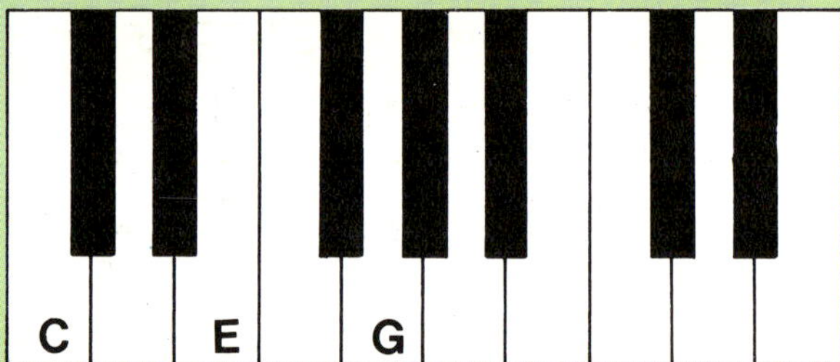

The simplest of all chords is made up of just three notes, each two tones apart. This is called a *triad.* The first note of the triad is called the *root,* the next the *third,* and the last the *fifth* (being the third and fifth notes of the chord, respectively).

Let's now take the chord of C major. Don't be afraid of the words *major* and *minor.* You'll find them cropping up all over the place in music. They merely describe the *mode* on which that particular scale is based (the arrangement or grouping of the rungs in that particular musical stepladder).

The root position is C, followed by E, and then G. There are two other ways in which you can play the same three notes. Note that the root can be in the top position, or in the middle.

Whichever way it is played, it is still the chord of C major, but played in different positions. Any position other than the root position is called an *inversion.*

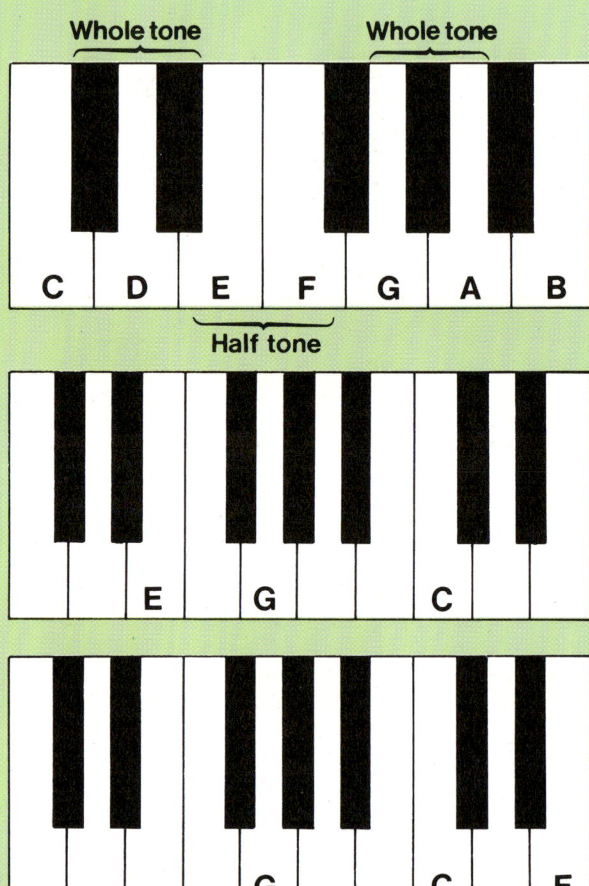

Right: *Keyboard session-man Billy Preston uses a vast range of electronic equipment.*

That was the major triad. In the minor triad the intervals are slightly different. It is really very similar to the major triad, except that you play D sharp instead of E, as in the three examples below:

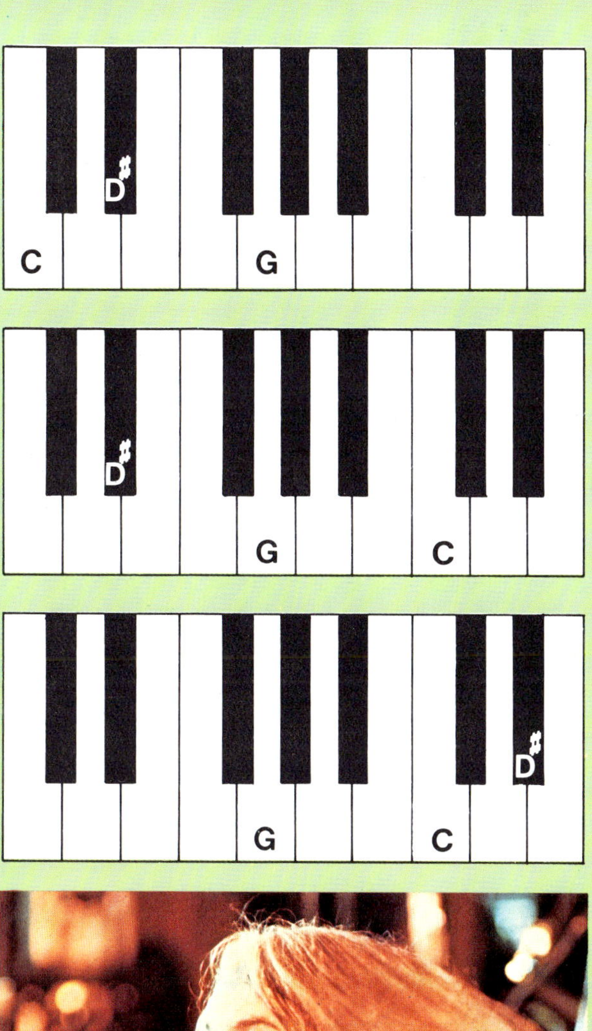

A *seventh chord* is made up of four tones. It is called 'seventh' because when played in the root position there are seven consecutive tones embraced by the chord. Any triad can be turned into a seventh merely by adding another interval above the fifth of the triad.

C major seventh adds an interval above the fifth of a major triad, and because there are four notes, there are four positions in which the chord can be played, like this:

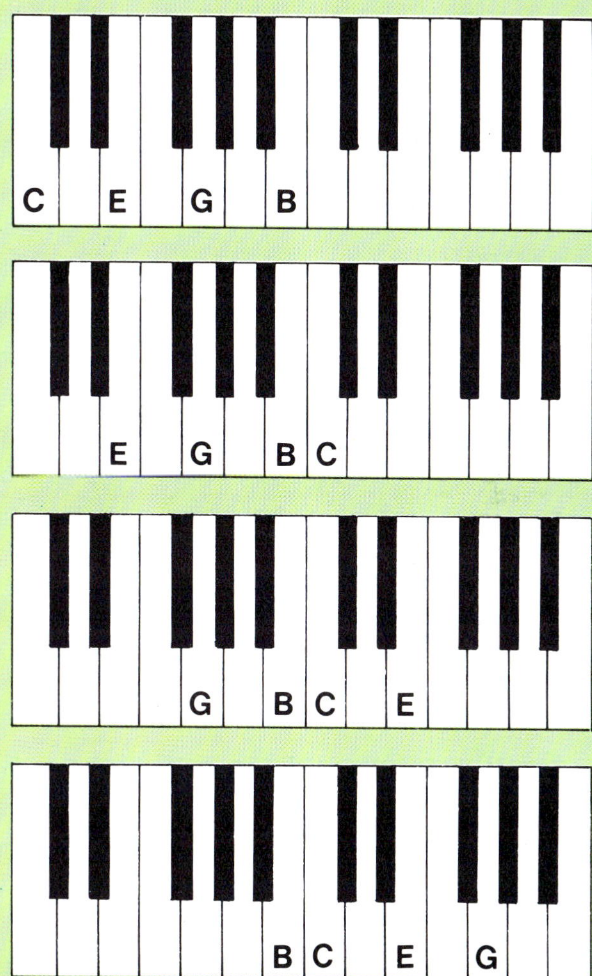

There are literally thousands of chords, most of which you will never need. You'll find some of the most useful ones in the chord chart at the end of this book. But once you learn how a chord is built up, you will be able to form your own chords for almost every occasion.

Left: *Although a multi-instrumentalist, Leon Russell is usually regarded as a keyboard player, and has formed his own band.*

HOUSE OF THE RISING SUN

The House of the Rising Sun became popular after both Bob Dylan and The Animals recorded it in the early 1960s. This piece is in F major, which means that you play B flat. From now on you'll be coping with three notes at once: these form what is called a *triad*.

Below: *Dave Rowberry of The Animals.*

																D
				A	D		E	F		A	G		D	D		
				1	2		3	4		5	4		2	2		5
				There	is		a	house		in	New		Or—	leans,		They
					A F D			C A F			D			F D		
											B♭ G			B♭		

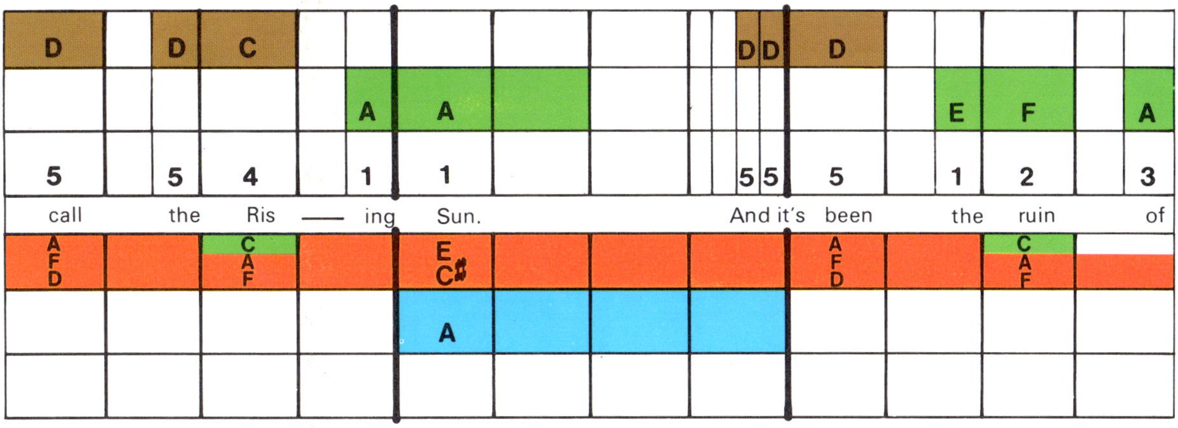

D		D	C							D	D	D					
					A	A								E	F		A
5		5	4		1	1				5	5	5		1	2		3
call		the	Ris	—	ing	Sun.				And it's		been		the	ruin		of
A F D			C A F			E C♯						A F D			C A F		
						A											

G	D	D	D	D		D	D		D	C♯		C♯	D			
2	1	1	1	1		1	1		1	2		2	1			
ma — ny		a	poor	boy,		And	God,		I	know		I'm	one.			
D				F D			A F D			E C♯			A F D			
B♭ G				B♭						A						

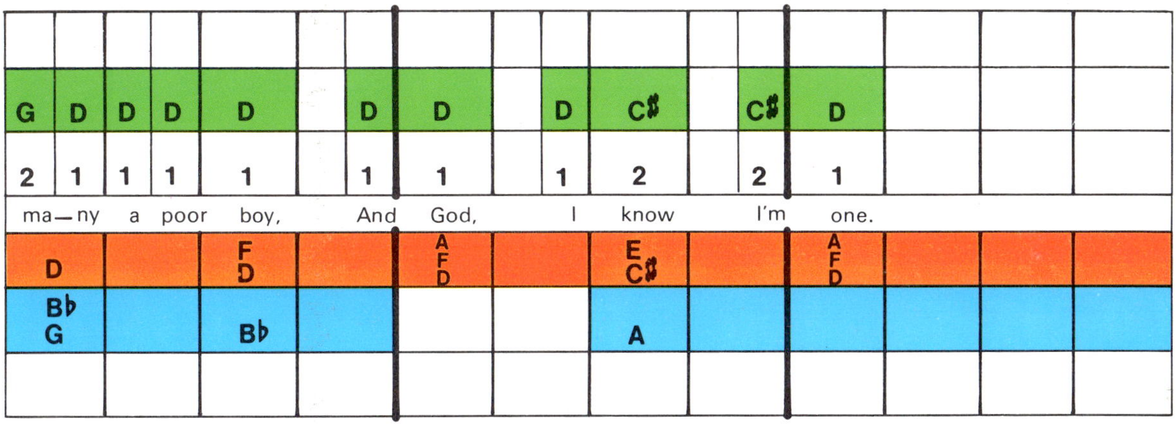

2. My mother was a tailor,
Sewed my new blue jeans.
My father was a gamblin' man,
Down in New Orleans.

3. Now the only thing a gambler needs
Is a suitcase and a trunk.
And the only time he'll be satisfied
Is when he's all a-drunk.

4. Oh! mother, tell your children,
Not to do what I have done.
Spend your lives in sin and misery,
In the house of the Rising Sun.

5. Well I've got one foot on the platform
The other foot on the train.
I'm going back to New Orleans
To wear that ball and chain.

6. Well, there is a house in New Orleans,
They call the Rising Sun.
And it's been the ruin of many a poor boy,
And God, I know I'm one.

Above: *The Animals gained their name from their wild acting on stage.*

THERE'S A KIND OF HUSH

THE CARPENTERS had a chart-topping success with *There's a Kind of Hush.*

The tune is in the new key of B flat major, which means that you play E flat and B flat.

Right and below: *The vocal artistry of The Carpenters has established them as major recording stars.*

												D	C			
			D	Eb	F		F	F	D Bb		F♯ C		A	Bb G	A F♯	G
			1	2	3		3	3	3 1		3 1	5	4 1	3 1		
			There's a		Kind		of	Hush				all	ov—	er	the world	
					Bb		F	Bb		D			D		F♯	

							D	C									
G	D Bb		G D	Ab	Ab	F D		Ab	Bb G	Ab F	G Eb	G Eb	G Eb	Eb	G Eb	Bb G	A F
			to-night.				All	ov—	er	the world			you	can hear the			sounds
G	D	G			Bb			Bb		D		Eb		Bb	Eb		Eb

C Eb D Eb C

A F | Eb C | A | A | Bb | Eb | D Bb | F | A F | D | Eb

of lov – ers in love, You know what I mean. Just the

F | C | F | A | Bb | F | Bb | Bb | F | F | F | A

D C

F | D Bb | F | D Bb | D Bb | F♯ C | A | Bb G | A F♯ | G | G | D Bb | G | Ab

two of us and no – bo – dy else in sight

Bb | F | Bb | Bb | D | D | F♯ | G | D | G

D C C

F D | Ab | Bb G | Ab F | G Eb | G Eb | Eb | G Eb | Bb G | A F | Eb C | A | A | Bb | Eb | Bb D

There's no- bo – dy else and I'm feel – ing good just hold – ing you tight.

Bb | Bb | D | Eb | Bb | Eb | Eb | F | F | F | A

C

Bb D | F D | F D | Ab F D | Bb | Bb G | G Eb | G Eb | Bb G | G

So lis — ten ve — ry care

Bb | F | Bb | D | Bb | Bb | Bb | D | Eb | Eb

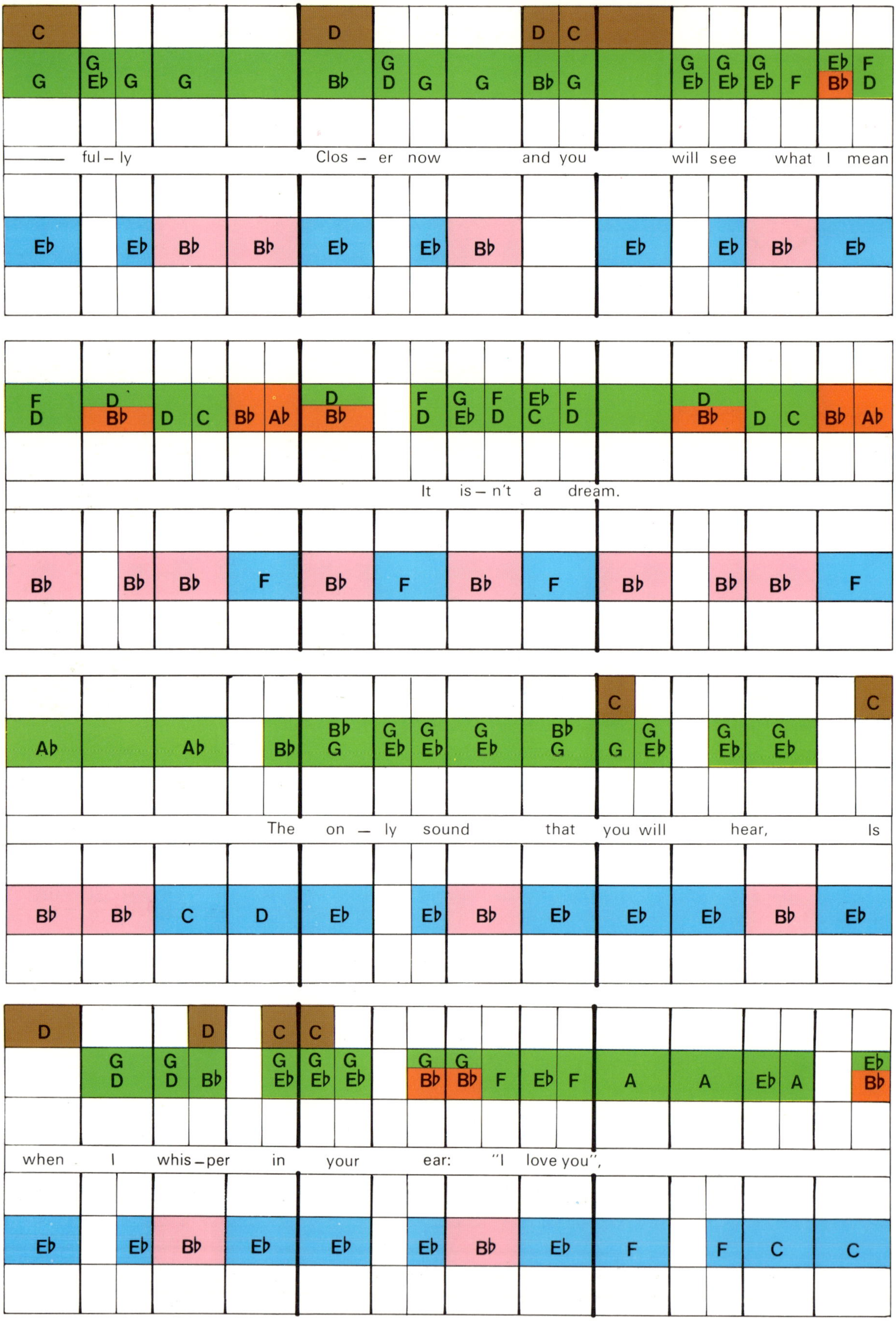

C D D C
G | G Eb | G | G | Bb | G D | G | G | Bb | G | G Eb | G Eb | G Eb | F | Eb Bb | F D
——— ful – ly Clos – er now and you will see what I mean
Eb Eb Bb Bb Eb Eb Bb Eb Eb Bb Eb

F D | D Bb | D | C | Bb | Ab | D Bb | F D | G Eb | F D | Eb C | F D | D Bb | D | C | Bb | Ab
It is – n't a dream.
Bb Bb Bb F Bb F Bb F Bb Bb Bb F

C C
Ab | Ab | Bb | Bb G | G Eb | G Eb | G Eb | Bb G | G | G Eb | G Eb | G Eb
The on – ly sound that you will hear, Is
Bb Bb C D Eb Eb Bb Eb Eb Eb Bb Eb

D D C C
G D | G D | Bb | G Eb | G Eb | G Eb | G Bb | G Bb | F | Eb | F | A | A | Eb | A | Eb Bb
when I whis – per in your ear: "I love you",
Eb Eb Bb Eb Eb Eb Bb Eb F F C C

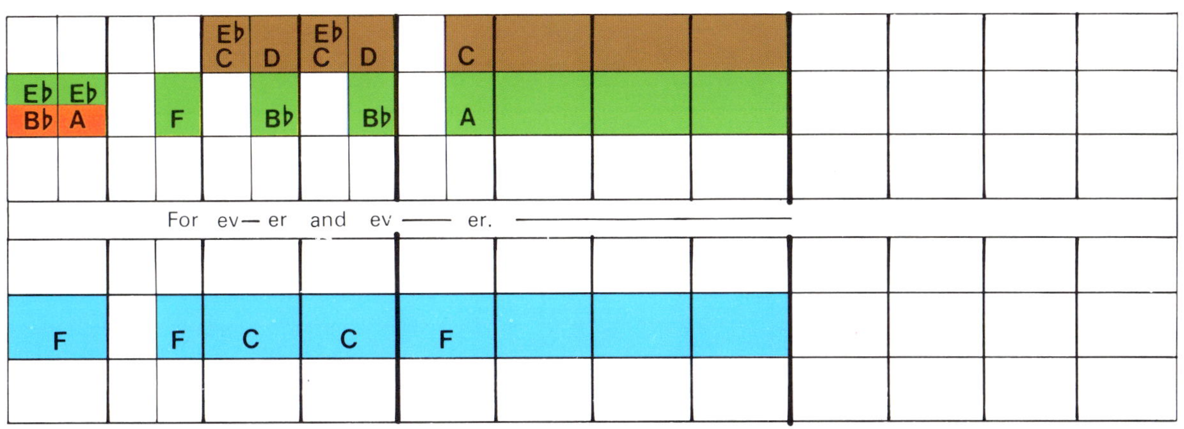

So listen very carefully,
Closer now and you will see,
What I mean,
It isn't a dream.

The only sound that you will hear,
Is when I whisper in your ear:
"I love you",
For ever and ever.

CHORUS:
There's a kind of hush,
All over the world tonight.
All over the world,
You can hear the sounds of lovers in love.

Right: *Richard Carpenter on electric piano.*

HOLDING A TUNE

MELODY AND *tune* are often regarded as meaning the same thing. But they're not quite the same.

A melody makes sense to the ear and some of it can be remembered. It might be described as 'a group of musical tones played one after the other to make a meaningful whole.'

A tune, on the other hand, is the kind of melody that can readily be recalled. When several instruments are being played, as in an orchestra, the melody that is most easily distinguished can be called the tune; but there are probably many other melodies being played at the same time.

A series of notes becomes a melody when it shows shape and pattern. But such notes do not have to move up or down the scale in a steady progression. They usually leap about from octave to octave.

An interesting feature that evolved from the advent of rock 'n roll in the 1950s was that the melodies were often made up of some of the older modes, instead of confining themselves to the conventional major or minor. As a result, some pieces were played using only the white notes of the keyboard. Various traditional 'rules' were broken or disregarded, and harmonies that sounded harsh, unpleasant, or 'not quite right' began to appear.

What else contributes to the making of a tune? Well, there is a thing called *harmony.* Harmony comes from the chords that are written in the vertical columns. Musically speaking, harmony is the study of chords and intervals, and their relationship to one another. The most important part of each chord is the *keynote,* which determines the key in which a piece is played. The keynote of a piece in C major, for example, would be C.

The basic interval on which chords are built is the *third.* In the chord of C major this would be E. The most important kind of chord is the *triad,* which you have already met.

It is possible, and often desirable, to change from one key to another in a piece of music. This is made possible by the fact that many chords are related to one another.

The end of a tune is usually signalled by a chord or chords that give the listener a sense of finality. This is almost always brought about by a chord that embodies the keynote of the piece. But the *first* note of a piece need not be the keynote, and quite often is not.

It is often quite difficult to tell whether a piece of music is being played in the major or minor mode. But as a rule, happy, tranquil music is likely to be in the major, while mournful music, with dark overtones, is likely to be cast in the minor.

Below left: *Composer David Bedford has worked with musicians such as Mike Oldfield and Kevin Ayers.*

Below: *Jon Lord, who has attempted to marry rock with classical music, is accompanied by the Royal Philharmonic Orchestra.*

Opposite: *Rock man Elton John is noted for his stage gear as well as his adept playing.*

SONS

NEVER COMES THE DAY

Never Comes the Day was written by Justin Hayward, of The Moody Blues. It was included in the album *On the Threshold of a Dream.*

Right: *Vocalist-guitarist Justin Hayward.*
Below: *The Moody Blues, best known for their 1960s hit single* Go Now.

E C	F♯ D	G E		E C	D B					E C	F♯ D	G E		A E	B
Work	a – way		——	to – day,		——				work	a – way		——	to – mor	
E	E		E	E		D			D	E	E		E	E	
G	G		G	G	G	G	G	G	G	G	G		G	G	G

B F♯	A	F♯	F♯	G E	F♯ D	G E		E	D	B	B	B	D B
——	row.	——		Nev —	er		comes	the	day	——			for
D♯		D♯	D♯	C		C	C			D		D	
B	B	B	B	G		G	G		G	G	G	G	G

my — love and me. — I feel her — gent — ly —

sigh-ing — as — the eve — ning — slips — a — way. — If

on — ly — you — knew — what's in — side of me now —

— You wouldn't want to know — me — some

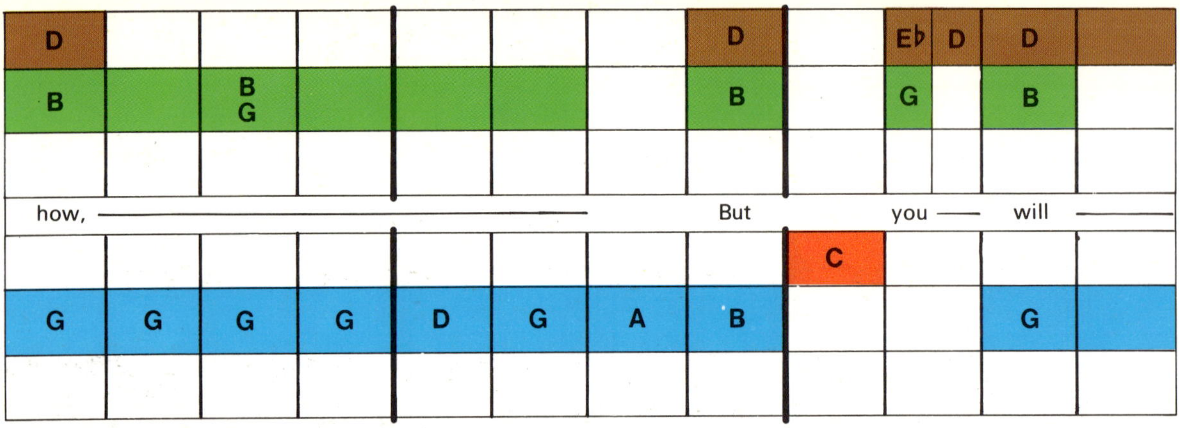

D							D		E♭ | D	D	
B		B G					B		G	B	
how, —							But		you —	will	—
								C			
G	G	G	G	D	G	A	B			G	

E♭ C | F♮ D	| E♭ C	D									
		B | B G			C E	B D | A C	G B	A C	B D	G B	
help me —	to —	night, —			We	all —	will	be	al —	right. —	
C				C	C						
		G				G	| G	D		G	

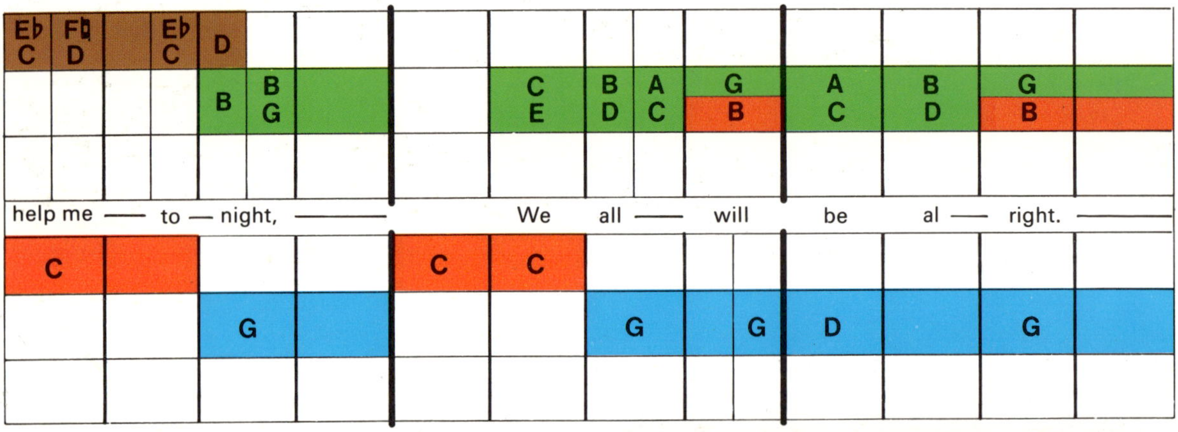

2. Give just a little more
Take a little bit less
From each other tonight.
Admit what you're feeling
And see what's in front of you,
It's never out of your sight.
We all know it's true,
You know it's true,
We all know it's true.

3. Work away today, think about tomorrow
(Then as 1st verse)

Above: *Mike Pinder made use of a Mellotron, which incorporated pre-recorded tapes.*

CONQUISTADOR

WRITTEN BY Gary Brooker and Keith Reid, *Conquistador* was recorded by Procol Harum at the beginning of the 1970s.

Once again you'll find yourself playing in B flat. This is a slow rock number so be sure you don't take it too fast.

Below: *Procol Harum were formed in the mid 1960s.*

	D	G D	B♭	A D	G	G D	B♭ E	B♭ E C	A E C	A E C	G E B♭			C	F	A F C		G	F	A F C
								5 3 1			5 3 1									
	Con-	quis-	ta –	dor,		your	stal-	lion	stands					in	need	of		com –	pa –	ny,

G			D	D♭	C			E	F	F			E	E♭

C
A F C | F C | F C | F C | F C | F C | F C | F C | D | G D | Bb | A D | G | G D | Bb E | Bb E C | A E C | G E Bb
5 3 1 | 5 3 1

And like some an — gel's ha – loed brow

D | G | A | Bb | D | Db | C | Eb | F

C | D | C | D | Eb
C | F | A F C | G | F | A F C | F C | F C | F C | A F C | A | Bb | A | B D | B D | B Ab D | A D | G D | F D | Eb
5 3 1 | 4 3 1

you reek of pu – ri – ty. I see your ar — mour plat – ed breast,

F | E | Eb | Eb | F | F♯ | G | G | G | A | B

C | Eb C | C | C | D | D | D | D
Eb | F | F | G | A C | A C | A Gb C | Gb C | A F C | Bb | E | Bb D

has long since lost its sheen, And

C | C | D | Eb
F | Bb | A | Ab | G | D | F | F♯

D | C | D | Eb | C | C | C | C | D | D | D | D
B D | B D | B Ab D | Ab D | G D | F D | Eb | Eb | G Eb | G Eb | G Eb | G Eb | G Eb | A C | Gb | F | Eb | D

in your death-mask face there are no signs which can be seen,

C | C | D | Eb
G | G | Bb | B | F | Bb | A | Ab

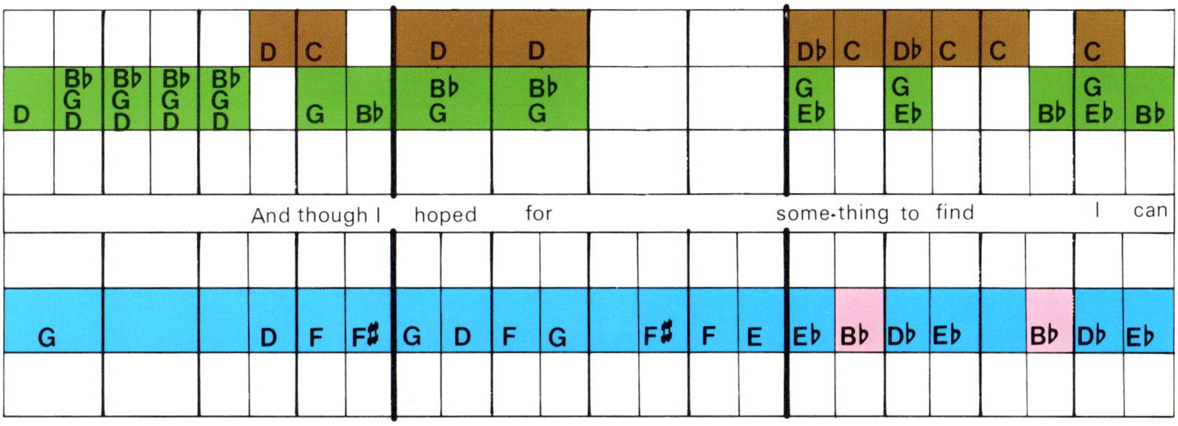

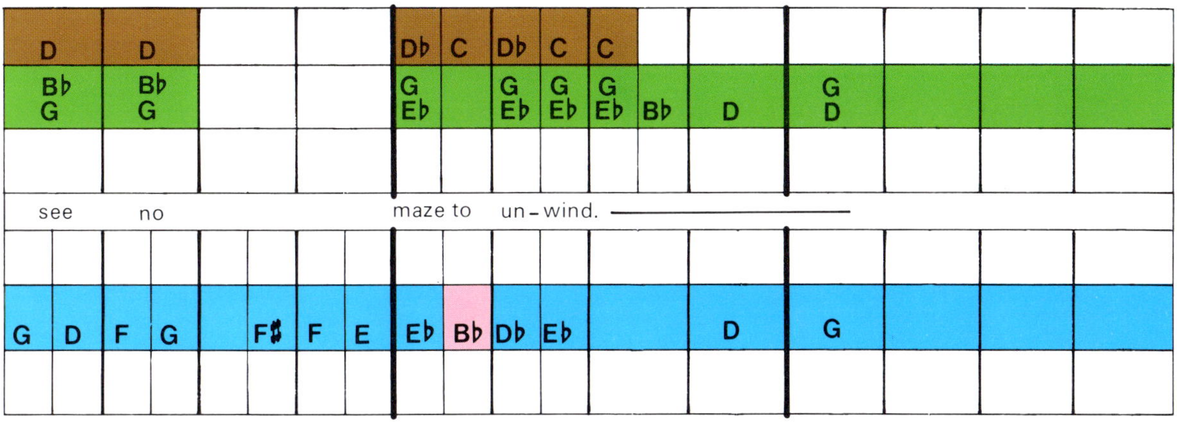

					D	C		D	D			Db	C	Db	C	C		C	
D	Bb G D	Bb G D	Bb G D	Bb G D		G	Bb	Bb G	Bb G			G Eb		G Eb			Bb	G Eb	Bb

And though I hoped for some-thing to find I can

G			D	F	F♯	G	D	F	G		F♯	F	E	Eb	Bb	Db	Eb		Bb	Db	Eb

D	D			Db	C	Db	C	C						
Bb G	Bb G			G Eb		G Eb	G Eb	G Eb	Bb	D	G D			

see no maze to un-wind. ———

G	D	F	G		F♯	F	E	Eb	Bb	Db	Eb		D	G				

2. Conquistador, your vulture sits upon your silver shield,
And in your rusty scabbard now the sand has taken seed.
And though your jewel encrusted blade has not been plundered still
The sea has washed across your face and taken of its fill.
And though I hoped for something to find
I can see no maze to unwind.

3. Conquistador, there is no time, I must pay my respect,
And though I came to jeer at you I leave now with regret.
And as the gloom begins to fall, I see there is no only all
Though you come with sword held high you did not conquer, only die.
And though I hoped for something to find
I can see no maze to unwind.

ACCOMPANIMENT: THE LOWDOWN

ACCOMPANIMENT IS musical material that supports the melody or voice. On the keyboard this may consist of bass (lower) notes and chords played with the left hand (usually) to accompany the melody in the right hand; or it may involve the use of both hands playing an accompaniment for another instrument that is looking after the melody. If the latter is the case, this does not mean that the keyboard becomes less important: its job there is to highlight the other instruments.

The keyboard, especially the piano, is often used on its own to accompany a singer. The singer sings the melody, so the keyboard plays either an accompanying harmony or some other accompaniment that does not include that particular melody.

IN the early 1960s, when the Beatles reigned supreme, the keyboard took a back seat and was used purely for accompaniment. But as the music gradually grew more complex, the keyboard came into its own once more, as featured in bands such as Pink Floyd. And in most jazz groups and in boogie, the piano has almost always been the main instrument.

Each style of music has its own particular kind of accompaniment. In boogie-woogie, for instance, the left hand usually digs into an almost mechanical pattern, repeated over and over again. Blues left hand playing is usually slow, with a steady, syncopated rhythm, while in jazz, the left hand often finds itself having to cope with a very complicated rhythm, even playing in a different time signature from that of the right hand.

You will find that some melodies can be adapted to a number of different bass accompaniments. Look at *Summertime,* for example, George Gershwin's classic blues. By keeping the melody in the right hand, you can play different bass accompaniments in the left. In other words, you have a choice and can decide which accompaniment you prefer.

Here are three different accompaniments for the left hand which you can try. The first has been widely used in all types of popular music, and has a very regular pattern of notes.

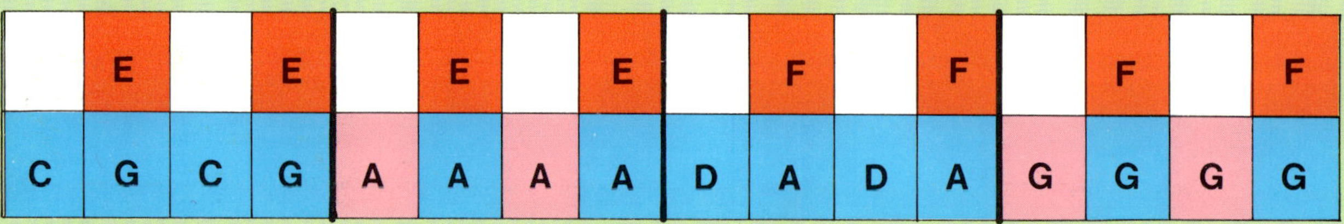

But playing the same notes over and over again in this way can soon become tiresome. Try varying the accompaniment to obtain a freer sound – like this:

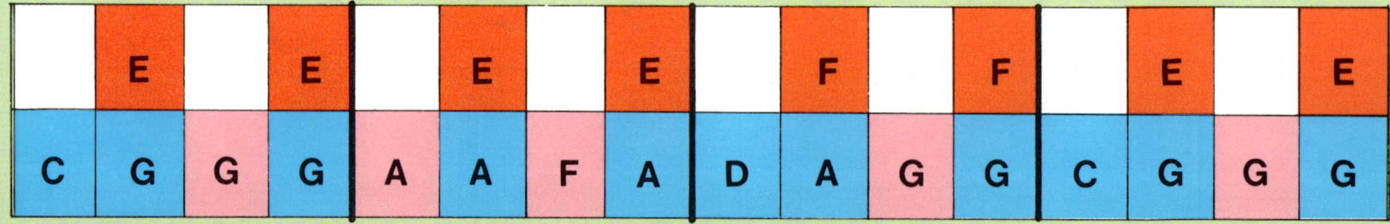

You can play some accompaniments an octave lower than indicated, to make them more interesting. When the melody moves rapidly, use a sustained accompaniment, with whole notes or half notes:

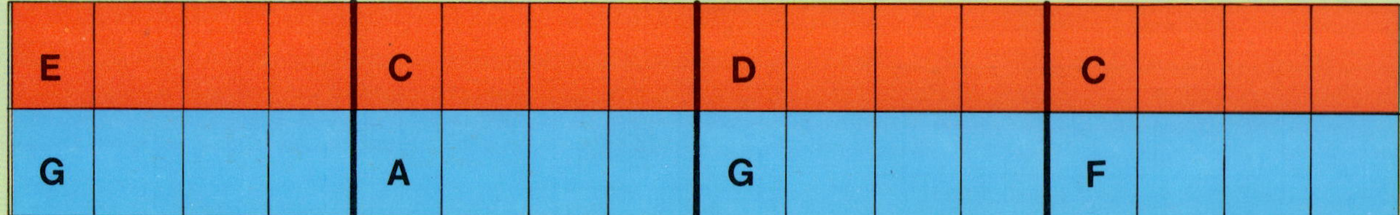

As you begin to get the hang of it, you will find that you can vary your left hand work quite naturally. Try combining the first two accompaniments you've just been shown, or alternate between the two. You will learn more about this in the chapter called *Use Your Ears – Improvise.*

A WHITER SHADE OF PALE

PROCOL HARUM had a tremendous hit with *A Whiter Shade of Pale* in 1967. The left hand plays a simple but effective bass run that has a rather classical feel to it. There are no sharps or flats that you need to worry about in this song.

Below: Procol Harum, photographed shortly after the release of A Whiter Shade of Pale.

Part	Notes (left to right)
Right hand (upper)	E C, D, E, D, D, C — C, D, D, D, C
Right hand (lower)	E C, G, A — A F C, A, A F, A
Lyrics	We skipped the light fan – dang – o … And turned cartwheels 'cross the
Left hand (upper)	C, C
Left hand (lower)	B, B, A, A, G, G, F, F, E, E

Part	Notes (left to right)
Right hand (upper)	C
Right hand (lower)	A, A, G, A, A, B G, B, A, A, A, G, G, F
Lyrics	floor. … I was feeling kind of sea – sick
Left hand (upper)	F, F, E, E, D, E
Left hand (lower)	D, D, C, D, E, F, G, G, A, B

C E D E C E C D C D
G E C G G A A B E A F C A A

But the crowd called out for more The room was humming

C C F E E
B B A A G F E F

C D C D
A F G D A A B G B A A A E G G G B

harder As the ceiling flew a — way

D D C D E F F F E E D
G G G A B

C D E D E E E G E E C C E E C D C D
G B B A B A F C A F A

When we called out for a – no — ther drink The waiter brought a

C C F E E
B B A A G F E F

E E G E E C E C E C E E C D C
A F C A F B G B G B A G

tray. And so it was that la — ter

D D C C
G G G B B A A G F E

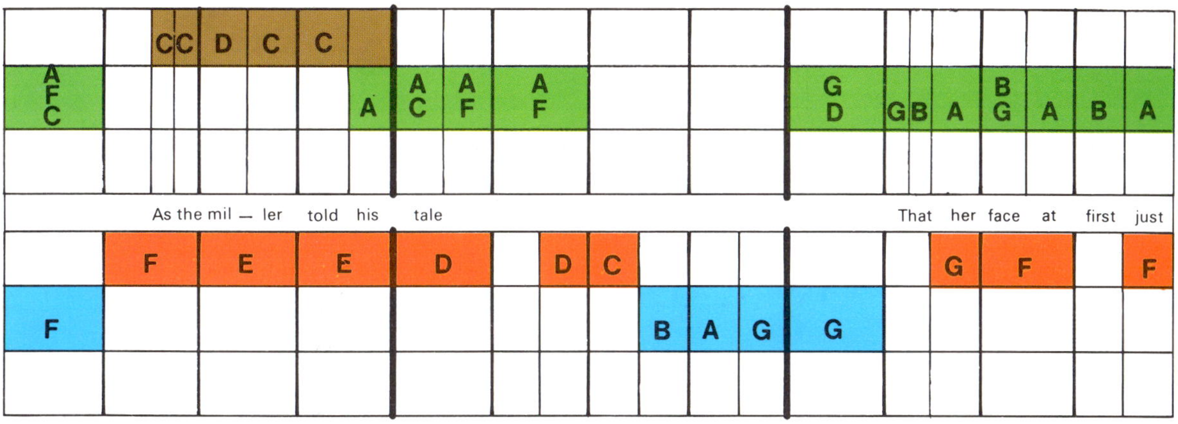

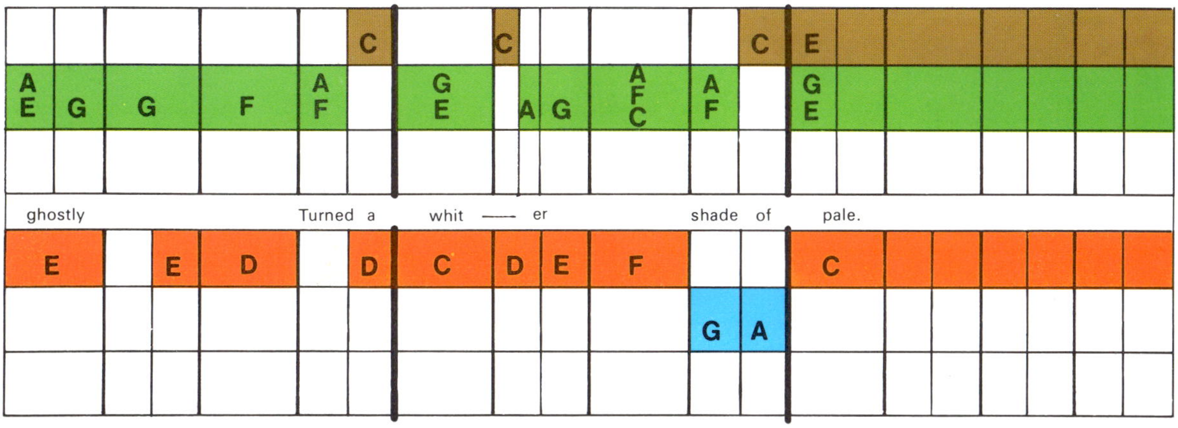

C C	D	C	C									
A F C				A	A C	A F	A F	G D	G B	A	B G	A B A

As the mil — ler told his tale That her face at first just

F	E	E	D	D	C					G	F	F
F						B	A	G	G			

				C	C		C	E
A E	G	G	F	A F	G E	A G	A F C	A F	G E

ghostly Turned a whit —— er shade of pale.

E	E	D	D	C	D	E	F			C
								G	A	

2. She said "There is no reason,
And the truth is plain to see",
But I wandered through my playing cards
And would not let her be
One of sixteen vestal virgins
Who were leaving for the coast.
And although my eyes were open
They might just have well been closed.

CHORUS:
And so it was that later
As the miller told his tale
That her face at first just ghostly
Turned a whiter shade of pale.

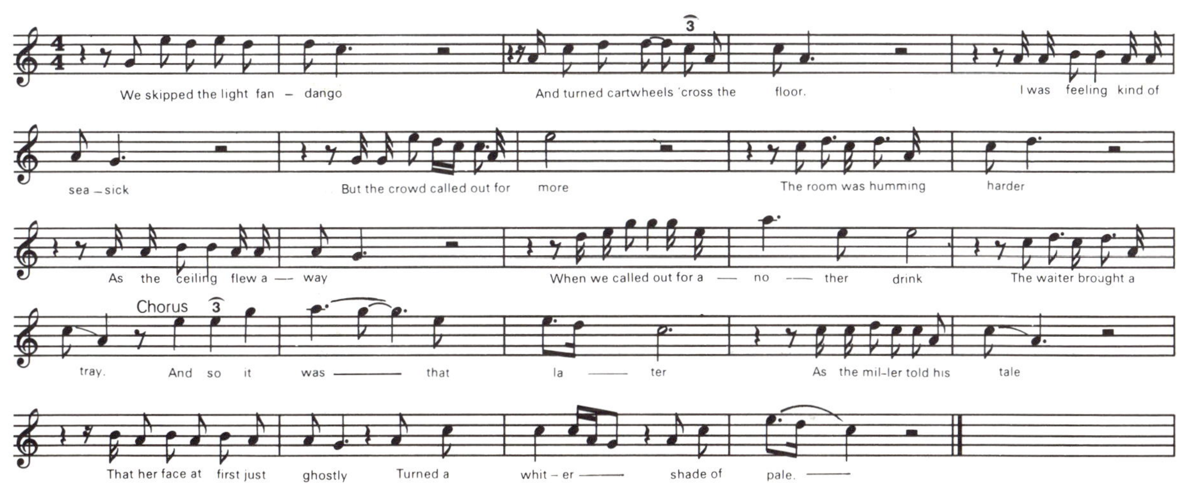

SCARBOROUGH FAIR

Scarborough Fair is a traditional song arranged by Simon and Garfunkel. This is in the new key of G major, which you'll see has an F sharp in it.

Above: *Simon and Garfunkel were a successful songwriting duo who parted in the early 1970s.*

E				E		B G	B G				B	F♯			G	F♯		E					
Are				you		go –	ing ———				to	Scar —			bor –	ough		Fair ———					
E	B	D	C♯	A	B	E	B	A	B	F♯	G	D	A	D	E	F♯	A	E	B	D	C♯	A	B

										D		E				D				C♯			
								B G		B		G				G		B G		A		A	
———								Pars –		ley,		sage,				rose –		mar –		y		and	
E	B	A	B	F♯	A	G	B	D	B	G	B	E	B	E	B	E	B	G	D	A	C♯	E	C♯

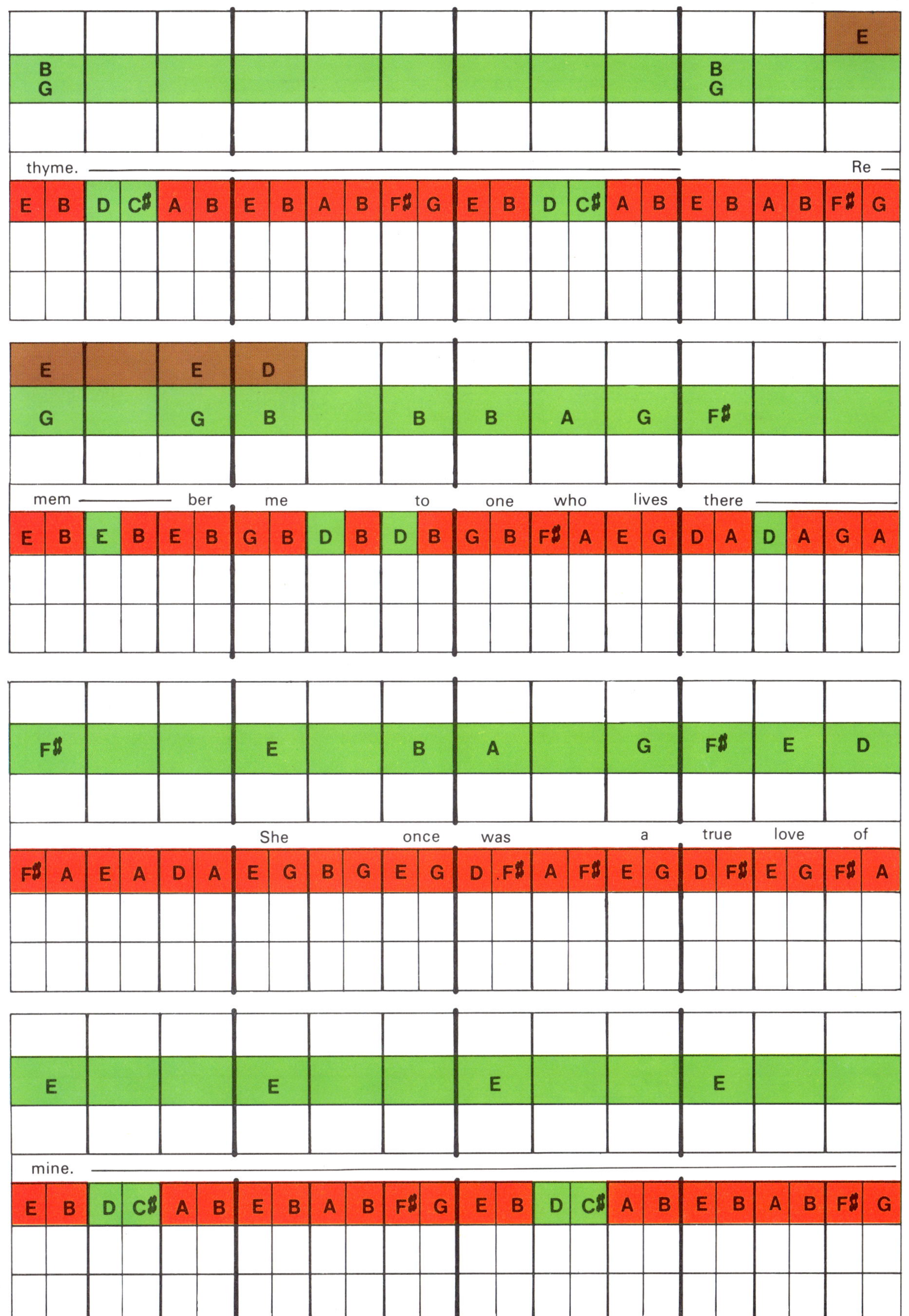
E
B G
B G
thyme. Re
E B D C♯ A B E B A B F♯ G E B D C♯ A B E B A B F♯ G
E E D
G G B B B A G F♯
mem ber me to one who lives there
E B E B E B G B D B D B G B F♯ A E G D A D A G A
F♯ E B A G F♯ E D
She once was a true love of
F♯ A E A D A E G B G E G D F♯ A F♯ E G D F♯ E G F♯ A
E E E E
mine.
E B D C♯ A B E B A B F♯ G E B D C♯ A B E B A B F♯ G

E	E	E	B E	B	B	F♯	G	F♯	E		

2. Tell her to make me a cam — bric shirt —

E	B	D	C♯	A	B	E	B	A	B	F♯	G	D	A	E	A	D	A	E	B	D	C♯	A	B

					D	E		D		C♯	
E				B G	B	G		G	B G	A	A

— Pars — ley, sage, rose — mar — y and

E	B	A	B	F♯	A	G	B	D	B	G	B	E	B	E	B	E	B	G	D	A	C♯	E	C♯

D	E	D	C♯	E	C♯	D	C♯	F♯	E		E
B				B				A	B		

thyme. — With

E	B	D	C♯	A	B	E	B	A	B	F♯	A	E	G	A	B	A	F♯	E	G	A	B	A	G

E		E	D								
G		G	B		B	B	A	G	F♯		

- out any seams nor nee — dle work

E	B	E	B	E	B	G	B	D	B	D	B	G	B	F♯	A	E	G	D	F♯	A	F♯	G	A

F♯			E		B	A		G	F♯	E	D
			Then		she'll	be		a	true	love	of

D	A	E	A	D	A	E	G	B	G	E	G	D	F♯	A	F♯	E	G	D	F♯	E	G	F♯	A

E			E			E			E		
mine. ———											

E	B	A	B	G	B	E	B	A	B	F♯	G	E	B	D	C♯	A	B	B E					

2. Tell her to find me an acre of land
   Parsley, sage, rosemary and thyme.
   Between the salt water and the sea strand
   Then she'll be a true love of mine.

CHORUS

3. Tell her to reap it with a sickle of leather
   Parsley, sage, rosemary and thyme.
   And gather it all in a bunch of heather
   Then she'll be a true love of mine.

CHORUS

Right: *Simon and Garfunkel in concert.*

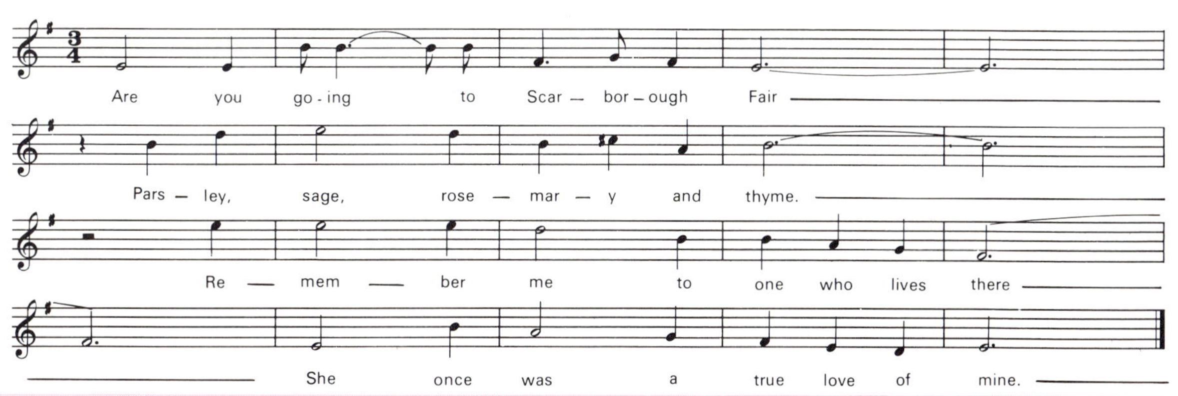

USE YOUR EARS–IMPROVISE

Above: *Stevie Wonder reached the top of the US single charts at the age of twelve, and has had a tremendous string of hits ever since.*

YOU ARE bound to be able to sing or hum or whistle a song from memory. You know which notes to use almost automatically, it seems. But when it comes to playing a tune from memory, that is not quite so easy. It's not your memory that's at fault; it's merely a lack of co-ordination between hands and ears. Obviously it helps to know the keyboard and how the notes will sound when played. Some find this easy, but everyone should be able to do it with practice, eventually.

Think of a simple tune that you know as well as the number on your front door. Now try to pick it out on the keyboard, using your right hand only. After just a few attempts you should have it spot on. It doesn't really matter which key you play it in, but as C major is the easiest you might as well start with that. With other keys, you'll find the black notes making a nuisance of themselves.

But even then, a well-known tune should not present you with too much difficulty.

'What about the left hand?' I hear you cry. Well, first of all, get the tune absolutely right every time with your right hand. Having done that you might try two or three chords with your left (refer to your chord chart at the end of the book) in the chosen key. Fool around with different chords until you find the one that seems to lie easiest with a particular note in the right hand. You don't need a chord for each note of the melody; one per bar would do. In this way you'll find that you have gradually worked out a simple tune in full on the keyboard entirely from memory.

Improvisation involves going a step further. Here you are not playing anything from memory. Instead, you are composing or inventing as you play. Admittedly this requires a certain amount of skill and is not achieved in a day. But improvisation becomes easier and more natural as your knowledge of the keyboard and expertise in playing progress.

You may improvise just a small passage or a complete piece of music. This holds particularly true for jazz where each musician in turn improvises for a few bars before returning to the main theme. Sometimes a group of musicians will improvise a whole composition, with none of them knowing what the others will play. If they play together regularly they will develop a kind of 'sixth sense' that will enable them to anticipate each other's musical contribution. On the other hand of course, playing together for the very first time, the results are rarely successful.

The first thing to remember about improvisation is that the music is continuous in time. In other words, it moves on, so that you have no time to stop and think. As you play one chord you must already have planned what the next one is going to be. At the same time you must not lose your sense of rhythm because that is the all-important factor. You can even improvise on one note, provided the note has a certain value. In this way you can have whole note, half note, whole note, whole note, and so on; and that type of arrangement is what provides the rhythmic pattern for all music. The first example shows this.

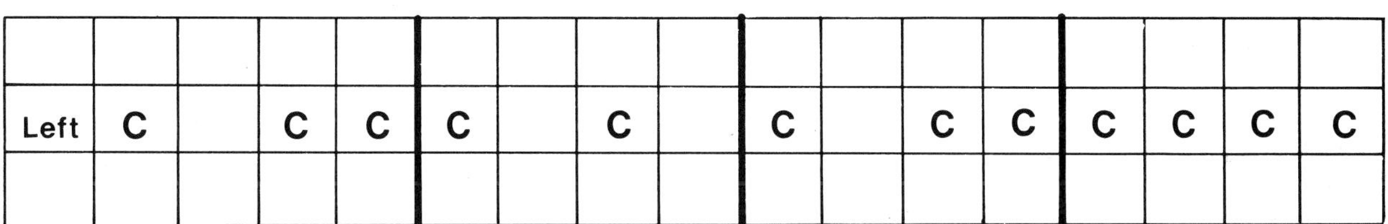

Left	C		C	C	C		C		C		C	C	C	C	C	C

Such a tune would no doubt bore the pants off you, but it does highlight the importance of rhythm.

Well, how do you start? First, decide which key you want to play in. As these will be only very simple tunes to begin with, you'd better stick to the keys you know: C major, G major, D major, and F major. When you have learned the notes that make up your chosen key, sit at the keyboard and play a few of those notes, in any order. Gradually some sort of melody will begin to struggle for recognition. Provided you stay within your chosen key you'll find that almost any notes will begin to form a tune. (This is all right-handed work, by the way.) As time goes on, various chords will come readily to mind and it is the knowledge of these and where they are likely to fit that really starts you improvising. All you need to do with your left hand is to provide a simple bass accompaniment. Let your right hand fingers do the walking!

The kind of bass line that regularly repeats itself is the easiest because then you don't have too much to remember. Try the second example of left hand accompaniment now.

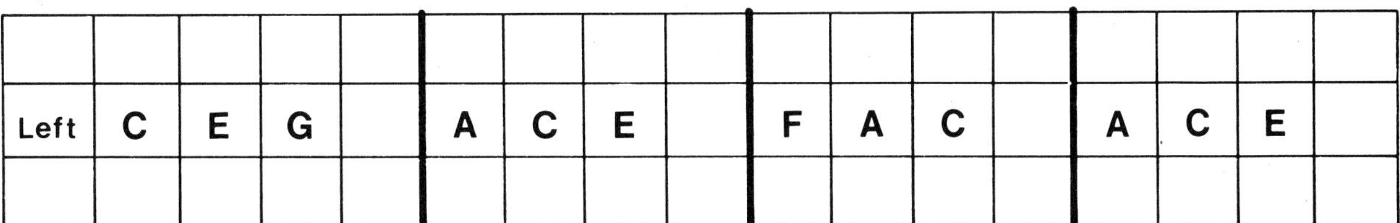

Left	C	E	G		A	C	E		F	A	C		A	C	E	

You can repeat this as many times as you like. Then try working out a similar pattern of your own. Improvisation can be great fun, especially when you're in a jam session with other instruments.

And now you're really on your own. You've learned to play a keyboard instrument and picked up some knowledge of music on the way. And the pleasing thing about it is that you've done it all by yourself. Hopefully you'll soon be the life and soul of the party. Play through the last three numbers in the book – and have fun!

BLUES IN D

Blues in D, written by Vanessa Lewendon, provides an introduction to improvisation. Learn the left hand first and become familiar with the chord progressions. This accompaniment can also be played without using the sharps – for example F instead of F sharp. Also try leaving out the middle note of each triad. After this, try experimenting with the right hand.

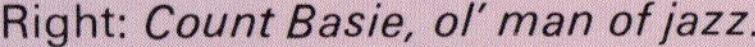

Right: *Count Basie, ol' man of jazz.*

	Bar 1	Bar 2	Bar 3
Right hand			
Left hand	E/C#/A E/C#/A F#/D/A F#/D/A G/E/A G/E/A F#/D/A F#/D/A	D/B/G D/B/G E/C/G E/C/G F/D/G F/D/G E/C/G E/C/G	A/F#/D A/F#/D B/G/D B/G/D C/A/D C/A/D B/G/D B/G/D

	Bar 1	Bar 2	Bar 3
Right hand	D F D C	D E F G# G F D C D F D	D E F G# A F G# A F D C
Left hand			

	Bar 1	Bar 2	Bar 3
Right hand			
Left hand	A/F#/D A/F#/D B/G/D B/G/D C/A/D C/A/D B/G/D B/G/D	A/F#/D A/F#/D B/G/D B/G/D C/A/D C/A/D B/G/D B/G/D	A/F#/D A/F#/D B/G/D B/G/D C/A/D C/A/D B/G/D B/G/D

	Bar 1	Bar 2	Bar 3
Right hand (upper)			C D D C D C
Right hand	D E F G A G F D F G# G	F D F F D F F D F F D F	A A A G# G F
Left hand			

	Bar 1	Bar 2	Bar 3
Right hand			
Left hand	D/B/G D/B/G E/C/G E/C/G F/D/G F/D/G E/C/G E/C/G	A/F#/D A/F#/D B/G/D B/G/D C/A/D C/A/D B/G/D B/G/D	E/C#/A E/C#/A F#/D/A F#/D/A G/E/A G/E/A F#/D/A F#/D/A

C D | D

G F G F G F G F G F G A G F D | D F G G# G F D C D F D | D E F D E F A

D D E/C E/C F/D F/D E/C E/C | C C | C C

B/G B/G G G G G G G | A/F#/D A/F#/D B/G/D B/G/D A/D A/D B/G/D B/G/D | A/F#/D A/F#/D B/G/D B/G/D A/D A/D B/G/D B/G/D

G# D C

D E F G G# A B A G F D | D F G G F D F E D C D | A/F/D A/F/D G/D A/D F/D D D

C C | C C | D D E/C E/C F/D F/D E/C E/C

A/F#/D A/F#/D B/G/D B/G/D A/D A/D B/G/D B/G/D | A/F#/D A/F#/D B/G/D B/G/D A/D A/D B/G/D B/G/D | B/G B/G G G G G G G

D F/D G/D G/D A/F/D A/F/D G/D G/D | A/G/E A/G/E A G E D# D C D E C | D E F G G# A G F D C D F D

C C | E/C# E/C# F#/D F#/D G/E G/E F#/D F#/D | D D E/C E/C F/D F/D E/C E/C

D/F#/A D/F#/A B/G/D B/G/D A/D A/D B/G/D B/G/D | A A A A A A A A | B/G B/G G G G G G G

D F/D G/D G/D A/F/D A/F/D G/D G/D | F D F D F D F D D C# D/A/F

C C | E/C E/C A

A/F#/D A/F#/D B/G/D B/G/D A/D A/D B/G/D B/G/D | A/F#/D A/F#/D B/G/D B/G/D A A F#/D

WHEN I'M DEAD AND GONE

When I'm Dead And Gone is a foot-tapping number recorded by McGuinness Flint. The syncopated rhythm makes the timing a little tricky. This tune is in D major.

Below: *McGuinness Flint were joined by Gallagher & Lyle, who wrote* When I'm Dead and Gone.

	F♯		E	D	D	D	D	D	D		D	D	D		D	
	A		G	F♯	F♯	F♯	F♯	F♯	F♯	B G	B	B	B	B G	B	B G
	Oh		I	love	you	ba	—	by,	I	love	you	night		and	day,	

																		D	
D		D	D	A	A	D		D	D	D	E	F♯	G		G	G			D

	G		F♯	E			F♯		E	D	D	D	D	D	D
	B		A	G			A		G	F♯	F♯	F♯	F♯	F♯	F♯
							When		I	leave	you	ba	—	by	don't

																			D	
G		G	G	G	F♯	E	D		D	D	D	A	A	G		G	G			D

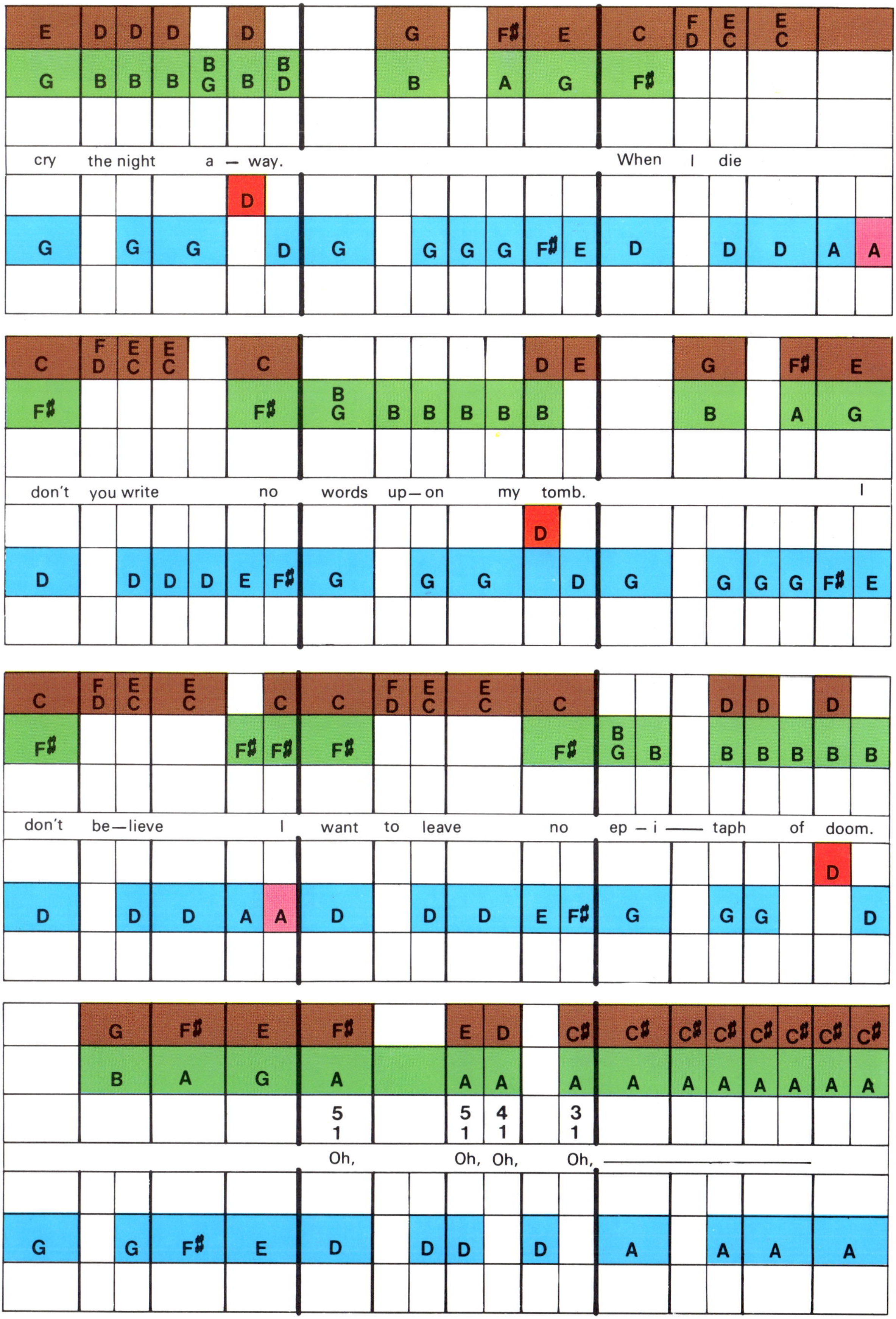

E D D D D | G F♯ E | C F/D E/C E/C
G B B B B/G B B/D | B A G | F♯

cry the night a — way. When I die

D
G G G D | G G G G F♯ E | D D D A A

C F/D E/C E/C C | D E | G F♯ E
F♯ F♯ | B/G B B B B B | B A G

don't you write no words up—on my tomb. I

D
D D D D E F♯ | G G G D | G G G G F♯ E

C F/D E/C E/C C | C F/D E/C E/C C | D D D
F♯ F♯ F♯ | F♯ F♯ | B/G B B B B B B

don't be—lieve I want to leave no ep — i —— taph of doom.

D
D D D A A | D D D E F♯ | G G G D

G F♯ E | F♯ E D C♯ | C♯ C♯ C♯ C♯ C♯ C♯ C♯
B A G | A A A A | A A A A A A A
5/1 5/1 4/1 3/1

Oh, Oh, Oh, Oh, ——

G G F♯ E | D D D D | A A A A

F♯ E D D D | D E D | F♯ F♯ G G F♯ E C♯

B B B B B F♯ B | B G B G B G B G B G B G | A A A A A A

When I'm dead and gone, I want to leave some hap-py wo–

B B B B | G G G G | D D D D

E C♯ E C♯ F♯ C♯ E C♯ D

A A A A A F♯

–man liv—ing on.

A A A A | D

2. Old Mama Linda she's out to get my hide,
She's got a shotgun and her daughter by her side.
Hey there Ladies, Johnson's free.
Who's got the love, who's got enough
To keep a man like me?

CHORUS:
Oh, Oh, Oh, Oh, – When I'm dead and gone,
Don't want nobody to mourn beside my grave.

Right: ***McGuinness Flint was formed jointly by Tom McGuinness from Manfred Mann and Hughie Flint from the John Mayall Band.***

THE ENTERTAINER

THE LAST piece is *The Entertainer,* written in 1902 by Scott Joplin.

The melody should be played through twice, substituting the end bar for the last bar of the melody on the second time around. The first three notes, on a *grey* background, should be played in the octave above the brown one.

Right: *Scott Joplin was a talented composer who wrote many ragtime pieces in the early 1900s.*

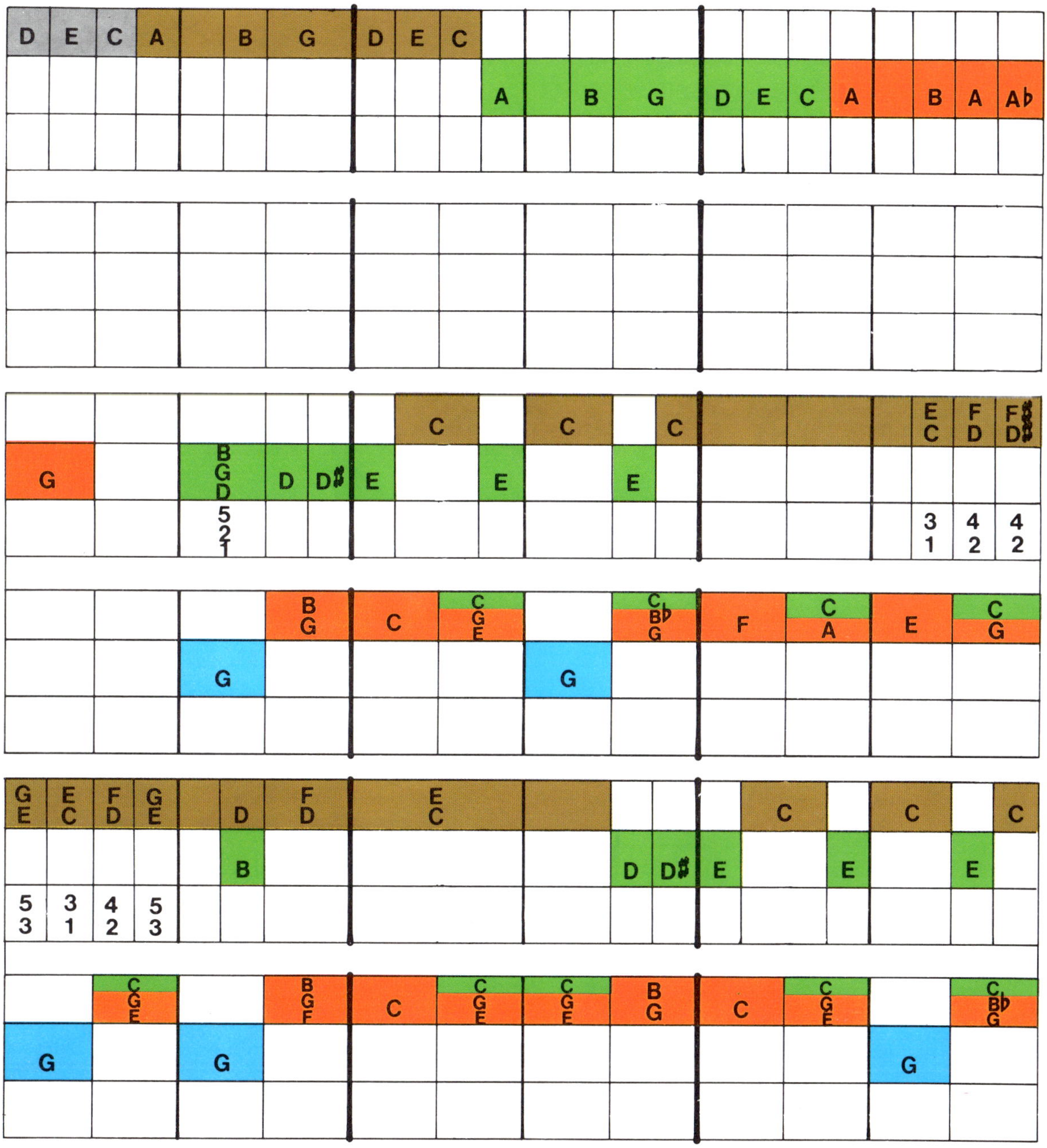

D	E	C	A		B	G	D	E	C												
										A		B	G	D	E	C	A		B	A	A♭

						C		C		C				E C	F D	F♯ D♯
G		B G D	D	D♯	E		E		E							
		5 2 1												3 1	4 2	4 2

			B G	C	C G E		C B♭ G	F	C A	E	C G
		G				G					

G E	E C	F D	G E		D	F D	E C					C		C		C
					B				D	D♯	E		E		E	
5 3	3 1	4 2	5 3													

	C G E		B G F	C	C G E	C G E	B G	C	C G E		C B♭ G
G		G								G	

						C	C			C	E		D	C		F/D							
						A	G	F♯	A						A							D	D♯
								2	1	3	5		4	3	2								
F		C/A		E		E♭		D		C/A/F♯		D		C/A/F♯		B/G		G		A		B	
																		G		A		B	

	C			C			C						E/C	F/D	F♯/D♯	G/E	E/C	F/D	G/E		D	F/D	
E			E			E															B		
C		C/G/E		G		C/B♭/G		F		C/A		E		C/G		G		C/G/E		G		B/G/F	

E/C						C	D	E	C	D	E		C	D	C	E	C	D	E		C	D	C
						1	2	3	1	2	3		1	2	1	3	1	2	3		1	2	1
C		C/G/E		C/G				C/C		C/G		B♭		C/G		A		C/A		A♭		C/A♭	
												B♭				A				A♭			

G/E	E/C	F/D	G/E		D/B	F/D		E/C								E/C				C			
														D	D♯					G/E			
5/3	3/1	4/2	5/3		3/1	4/2		3/1															
G		C/G				B/G		C/G		G		A		B		C/G				C			
G				G						G		A		B						C			

CHORD CHART

HERE ARE the piano chords most often used in modern songs. You can refer to the chart when you want to work out your own arrangement of a song, or when you are accompanying other instruments such as the guitar. Remember that you can play the chords in any octave (high or low) depending on the sound you want to obtain.

Don't worry if the chord is not always in the root position because it is possible to play each chord starting with any of its notes.

A

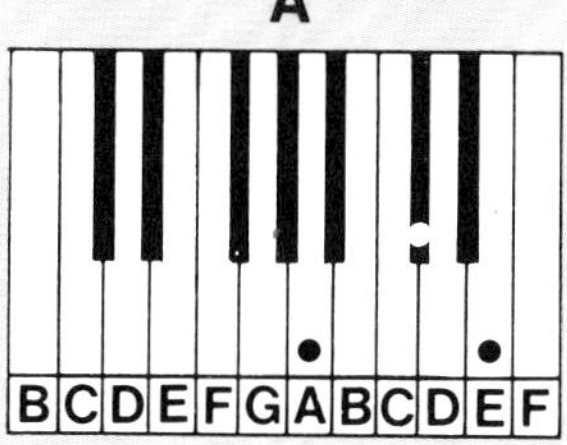

B

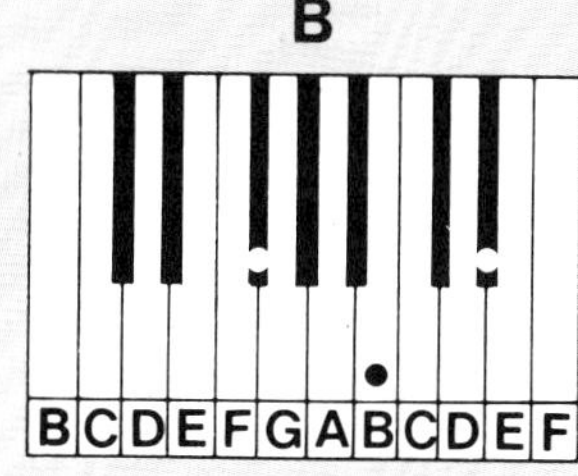

C

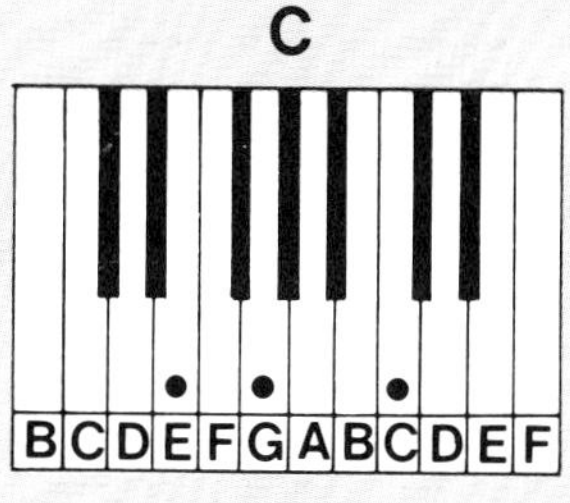

Am

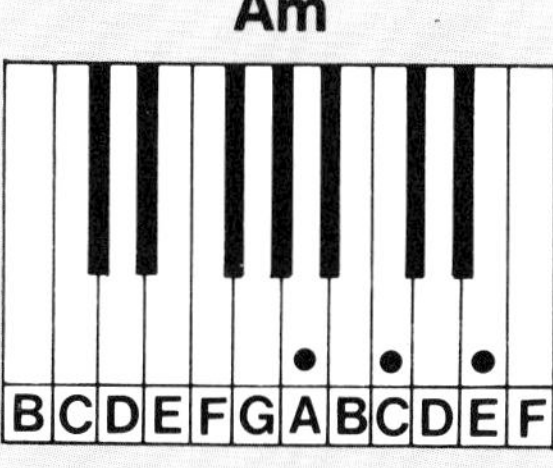

Bm

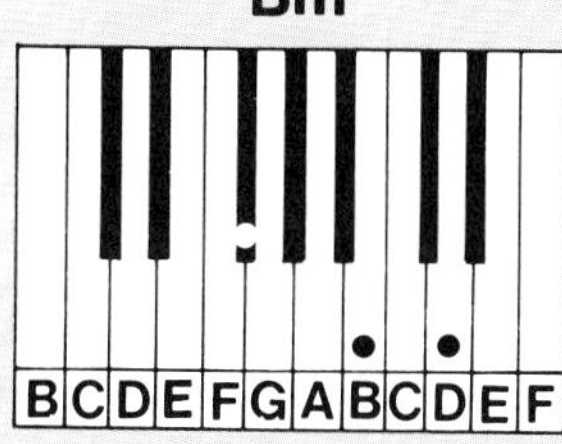

Cm

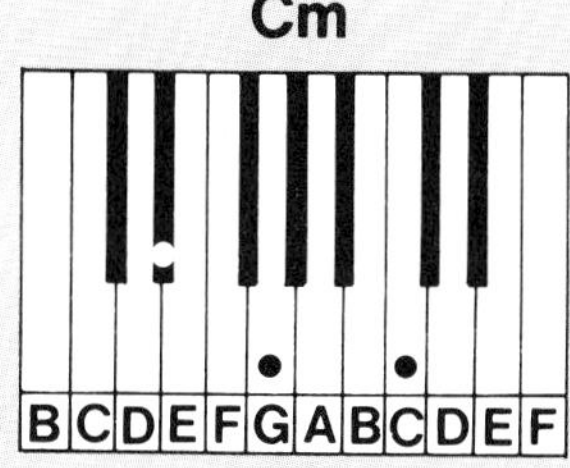

A7

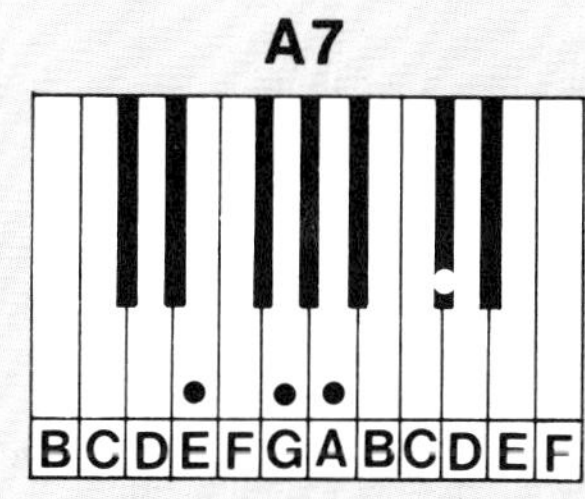

B7

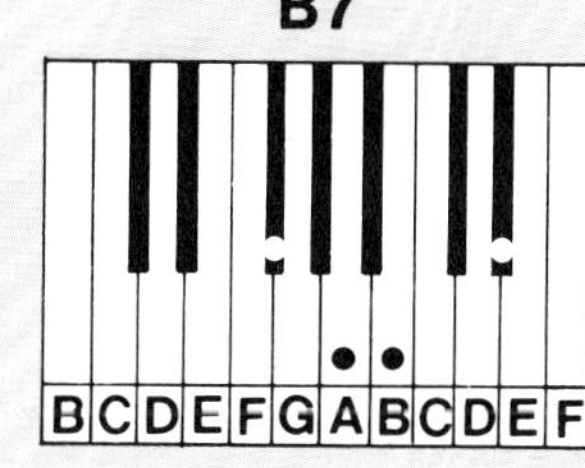

C7

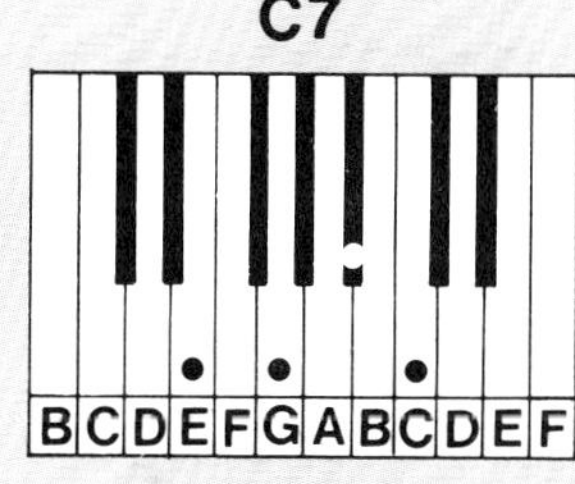

Am7

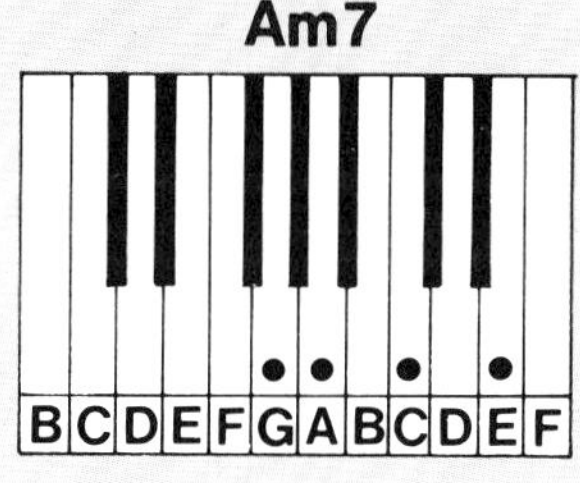

Bm7

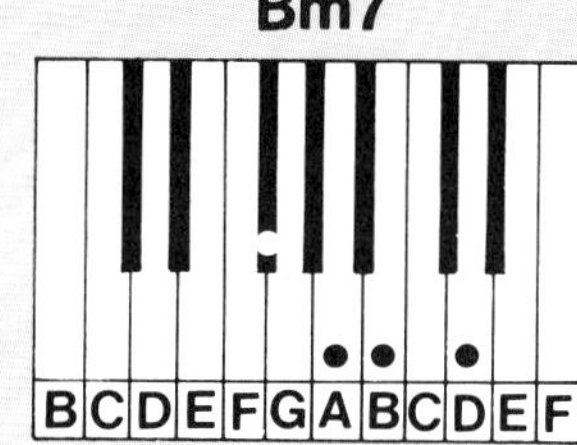

Cm7

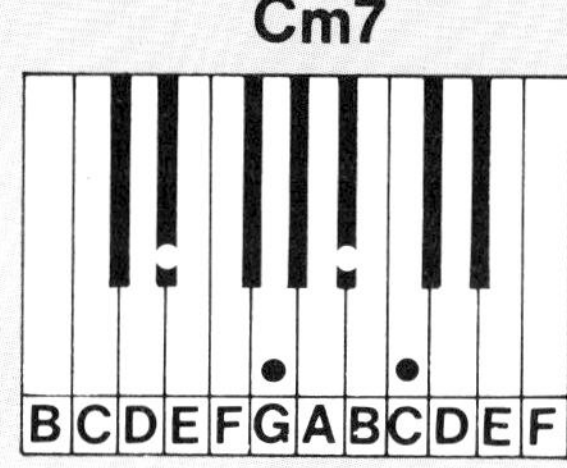

AM7

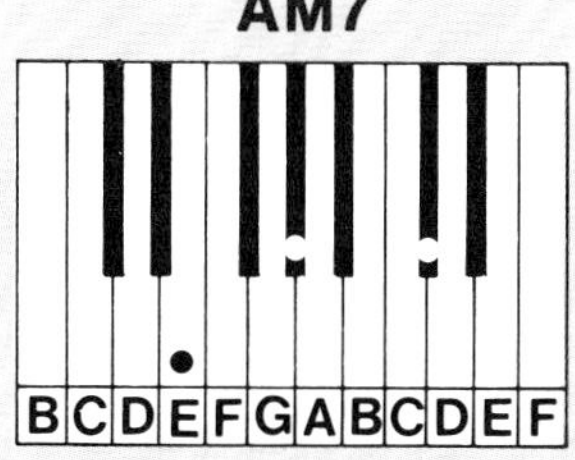

BM7

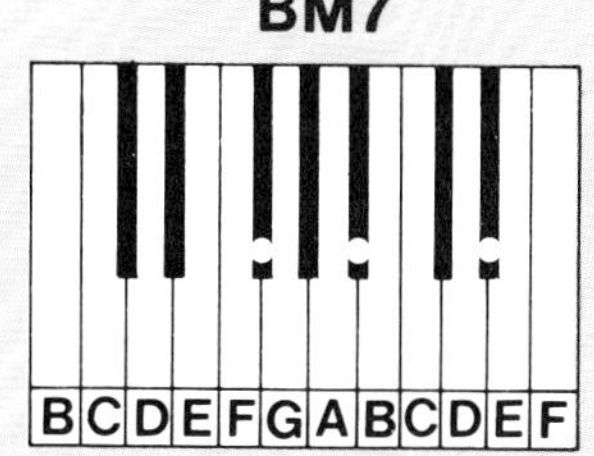

CM7

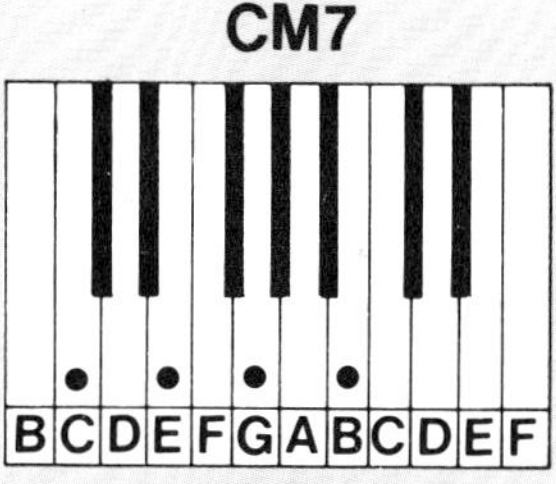

Adim7

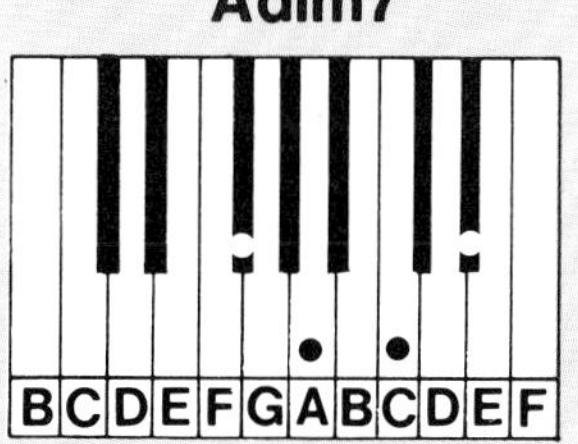

Bdim7

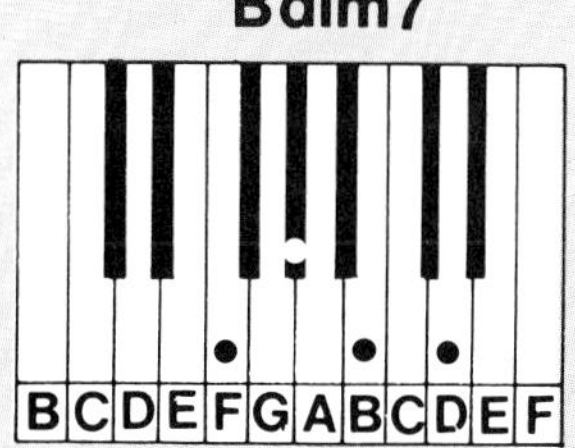

Cdim7

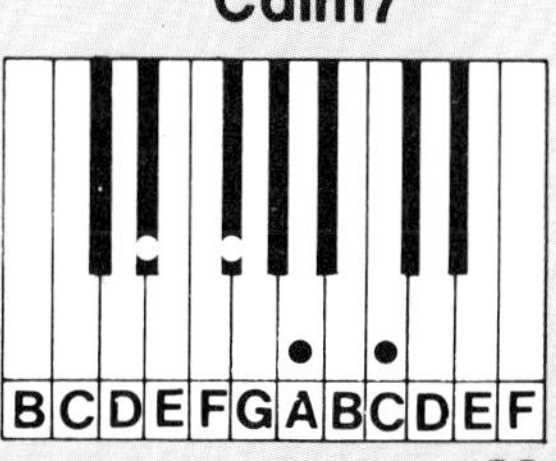

Published by The Hamlyn Publishing Group Limited; London ● New York ● Sydney ● Toronto ● Astronaut House, Feltham, Middlesex, England. ISBN 0 600 37201 4.